OUR COUNTRY'S
FIRST LADIES

OUR COUNTRY'S
FIRST LADIES

☆

Ann Bausum

WITH A FOREWORD BY
FIRST LADY LAURA BUSH

TABLE OF CONTENTS

President George W. Bush and First Lady Laura Bush (above) are the latest couple in a tradition of presidential partnership that dates back to 1789. From the time of George Washington on, a spouse, friend, or relative has served the nation alongside the President.

Laura Bush

ONE OF MY FAVORITE FIRST LADIES, Lady Bird Johnson, said, "The Constitution of the United States does not mention the First Lady. The statute books assign her no duties; and yet, when she gets the job, a podium is there if she cares to use it." Over the last two hundred years, America's First Ladies have stepped up to the podium to help shape the Presidency and the nation.

Abigail Adams, wife of the first President to live in the White House, was one of her husband's greatest political advisors. President Polk also relied on the political astuteness of his wife, Sarah, who even edited her husband's speeches. As official hostess of the White House, Julia Tyler, who was dubbed "the Presidentress," arranged for a reporter to cover social gatherings there so all the world could read about them. This reporter was essentially the first press secretary of the White House. Caroline Harrison pursued her own causes as First Lady, including raising money for a local university, but only after the school agreed to accept women students.

Edith Roosevelt oversaw one of the most significant renovations of the White House. In 1902 the West Wing was built to separate the executive offices from the family's living quarters, where Edith and President Theodore Roosevelt lived with their six children. Edith Wilson was one of her husband's most trusted advisors. She was the first presidential wife to make an overseas trip with the President. Lou Hoover made the first radio broadcast by a First Lady from the White House. In 1931, she urged thousands of women to donate food and clothing to needy families. Another social activist, Eleanor Roosevelt, spent twelve years as First Lady fighting for civil rights while her husband, Franklin D. Roosevelt, was President.

Given their popularity with the public, many First Ladies have campaigned in support of their husbands. On campaign stops, Harry Truman would ask supporters if they wanted to meet the boss. His wife Bess would emerge to the delight and applause of the crowds. Lady Bird Johnson even had her own train, the Lady Bird Special, and made the first independent whistle-stop campaign by a candidate's wife. The First Lady who inspires me the most is, of course, my mother-in-law, Barbara Bush. I have relied on her advice and guidance for years, and especially since I came to the White House. A lover of books and reading, she used her podium to increase awareness for family literacy and continues to support programs to combat illiteracy today.

The stories of our First Ladies are a vivid reflection of American history, and they deserve to be shared and remembered. Abigail Adams once reminded her husband to "remember the ladies." Through *Our Country's First Ladies*, the history of America's First Ladies will continue to be told, one remarkable woman at a time.

Laura Bush

Laura Bush
FIRST LADY OF THE UNITED STATES

About the First Ladies

AN INTRODUCTION

WHEN GEORGE WASHINGTON became the first President of the United States, he began setting the precedents, or customs, that would be followed by future Chief Executives. His wife Martha took on the same responsibility for the Presidents' spouses. Every presidential couple since then has added new touches to the roles of President and First Lady, or discarded old ones when they became out of date. More than 200 years after Washington's Presidency, the nation's First Family continues to observe traditions set during his administration and by those that have followed.

Among the customs that have evolved during the nation's 43 presidential administrations are some of its most famous terms. No one thought to call the President's partner the First Lady until the Buchanan administration, for example. The suggestion of "Marquise" was discarded. Early forms of address were "Presidentress," "Mrs. President," and "Lady." "First Lady" did not come into widespread use until the 20th century. It took more than a century for the official family residence to take on its classic name of the "White House,"

too. (Theodore Roosevelt gets credit for this term.) Earlier names were the "President's Palace" or, simply, the "President's House."

During their service, First Ladies have established traditions: Caroline Harrison, for example, introduced the first Christmas tree to the White House. They have coped with inquisitive reporters: Frances Cleveland went so far as to establish a private residence near the White House to serve as a family retreat. They have set examples by their actions: Eleanor Roosevelt resigned from the Daughters of the American Revolution to protest the group's discrimination against Marian Anderson, an African-American vocalist. They have indulged personal habits in private—Dolley Madison used snuff, for example—and weathered personal tragedies in public—Jacqueline Kennedy grieved on national TV after her husband was assassinated. They have faced unfavorable publicity—from disclosures about Mary Todd Lincoln holding séances to Nancy Reagan consulting with an astrologer. Two of them—Abigail Adams and Barbara Bush—have even raised sons who would grow up to become President.

The duties of First Lady come without the benefit of a job description or the reward of a paycheck. It is a position gained through personal ties to the President, whether it is wanted or not. Some First Ladies—including Mary Todd Lincoln and Helen Taft—were eager for the post and even pushed their husbands toward the Presidency. Others—like Jane Pierce and Margaret Taylor—despised the idea so much that they prayed for election defeats. Willing or not, they moved into the White House.

This book profiles the 44 women most often recognized as our country's First Ladies. With the exception of Harriet Lane, niece of James Buchanan, all of them were married to Presidents, either before or during their administrations. The stories told here may focus on 44 individuals, but they mirror the lives and times of their peers from the full span of U.S. history, offering readers a glimpse of the world both within and beyond the confines of the White House.

The earliest First Ladies, like all women from that time, had few educational opportunities. What schooling they had came at home. Many were in second marriages, because in that era death often brought a premature end to marriage. Children were frequently lost at early ages, too. Personal details for First Ladies—including lists of surviving children, names of non-presidential spouses, and ages at key life moments—are listed in fact boxes that accompany their profiles. Periodic timelines highlight key moments from women's history and summarize the evolving role of First Lady.

Abigail Adams, the nation's second First Lady, summed up feelings about the role of political spouse that many of those who followed her would share. "I feel a pleasure in being able to sacrifice my selfish passions to the general good," she noted. Abigail explained that sharing a life of public service "has taught me to consider myself and family but as the small dust of the balance, when compared with the great community."

The honor of service lasts a lifetime for First Ladies, just as it does for Presidents. Former presidential couples gather during times of sorrow, such as state funerals, and for happier occasions (above). Former First Ladies (from left) Rosalynn Carter, Barbara Bush, Betty Ford, Nancy Reagan, and Hillary Rodham Clinton gathered in 2003 to celebrate 20 years of drug and alcohol rehabilitation work by the Betty Ford Center.

FOUNDING
MOTHERS

★ *1789 – 1829* ★

1792

The publication of Mary Wollstonecraft's Vindication of the Rights of Women *sparked interest by U.S. women in such rights as property ownership, divorce, child custody, and voting.*

1805

Mercy Otis Warren brought scenes from the Revolutionary War to life (above) with the publication of her three-volume History of the Rise, Progress, and Termination of the American Revolution.

1805–1806

Sacagawea, a displaced Shoshone Native American, joined the Lewis and Clark expedition. Her knowledge of local peoples, places, and survival skills helped assure the success of the expedition.

1807

New Jersey revoked the right of women to vote. Not until 1893 would any state (Colorado) permit women to vote. Only 14 other states added this right before 1920.

Just as the first Presidents helped define their job description, the first Presidents' wives shaped the role that became known as First Lady. They developed social customs, established lifestyles in presidential mansions, influenced political affairs (from behind the scenes), and set the tone for social interactions with other governments. The first presidential spouses brought considerable experience to these tasks, having partnered with their husbands during diplomatic service and the Revolutionary War. Widowed Presidents recruited substitute hostesses to help them entertain.

1813

The nation's first textile mill was established in Waltham, Mass., initiating the employment of thousands of young women in factories.

1819

Emma Hart Willard presented "A Plan for Improving Female Education" to the New York State legislature. Two years later she founded Troy Female Seminary.

1824

Officials in Worcester, Mass., opened the nation's first public school for girls. New York State followed suit in 1826.

1828

Frances Wright was credited as the first woman to speak in the U.S. at a public gathering that included men in the audience. Her topic was the need for women's education.

Martha Washington

THE WASHINGTON ADMINISTRATION ★ 1789 – 1797

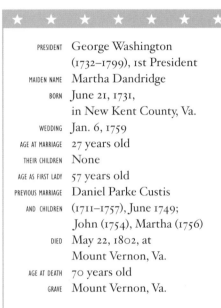

PRESIDENT	George Washington (1732–1799), 1st President
MAIDEN NAME	Martha Dandridge
BORN	June 21, 1731, in New Kent County, Va.
WEDDING	Jan. 6, 1759
AGE AT MARRIAGE	27 years old
THEIR CHILDREN	None
AGE AS FIRST LADY	57 years old
PREVIOUS MARRIAGE AND CHILDREN	Daniel Parke Custis (1711–1757), June 1749; John (1754), Martha (1756)
DIED	May 22, 1802, at Mount Vernon, Va.
AGE AT DEATH	70 years old
GRAVE	Mount Vernon, Va.

Did You Know?

• Martha Washington received so many sympathy letters following the death of George Washington that the U.S. Congress granted her "franking privileges," or the right to free postage, for her replies. That courtesy has been extended to 19 other presidential widows including, Dolley Madison, Mary Todd Lincoln, and Jacqueline Kennedy.

"A most becoming pleasantness sits upon her countenance.... [She is] the object of veneration and respect."

— Abigail Adams, 1789

WHEN GEORGE WASHINGTON BECAME the first President of the United States, Martha Washington gave no thought to remaining at their Mount Vernon home while he served. Although some future First Ladies would think twice before moving to the nation's capital (Rachel Jackson may even have had a heart attack and died rather than leave home), Martha did not hesitate. She had, after all, followed her husband to various army outposts during the Revolutionary War, and she was not about to desert him now. Martha did not hesitate to serve as a visible partner during Washington's Presidency either, a show of boldness that would be absent in some of the First Ladies who followed her. Thus the nation's first Presidency began not only with the leadership of a strong Chief Executive, but with the confident presence of his spouse, too.

Martha had grown up years before the formation of the United States. During her childhood she and everyone around her were subjects of the royal crown of England. Her father was planter John Dandridge. Her mother was named Frances Jones Dandridge. When she was 18 years old, Martha married Daniel Parke Custis, a wealthy plantation owner. She bore him two children who lived beyond infancy (two others did not). When Custis died eight years into their marriage, she became one of the wealthiest widows in Virginia.

So many portraits portray Martha Washington during the final years of her life (left page), that it takes a scene from an earlier age (above) to remind viewers of the fullness of her life. Martha served as wife, mother, grandmother, plantation manager, army spouse, and presidential partner, among other roles. When at home with George Washington she was known as "Dear Patsy," but to the new nation of the United States she became "Lady Washington." Her capable service as the first First Lady set the stage for the women who followed her.

> "I have learned from experience that the greater part of our happiness or misery depends upon our dispositions, and not upon our circumstances."
>
> — Martha Washington

Two years later she married George Washington, who was by then a noted veteran of the French and Indian War. She was petite, a full foot shorter than the six-foot, two-inch-tall future President.

The earliest years of their marriage predate the turbulent Revolutionary War era. The couple raised Martha's children and managed their combined properties. During the Revolutionary War, Martha joined General Washington at his winter Army encampments. "Lady Washington," as she was called even then, darned soldiers' socks, organized relief efforts, and tended the sick. "Whilst our husbands and brothers are examples of patriotism, we must be patterns of industry," she explained.

Following the war, the couple returned to their plantation lifestyle at Mount Vernon. The evolving needs of the new nation brought the noted Revolutionary War hero out of this retirement, and by 1789 he had been named the country's first President. New York City hosted the earliest national capital. Washington took the oath of office there on April 30, 1789. By the end of May, Martha had joined him at the rented homes that would serve as office and residence for the new Chief Executive. Later the pair would move with the government to another temporary home, this time in Philadelphia. She and Washington are the only presidential couple who did not live at the executive mansion now known as the White House. (It was still being built during Washington's Presidency.)

The new President and his wife worked to establish traditions and ceremony to suit their new roles. Various forms of address were considered for both of them, with "Lady Washington" becoming the preferred title for Martha. The Chief Executive was addressed simply as "Mr. President" in a tradition that continues to this day. The two collaborated on how best to dress, entertain, and behave. It was important to set a tone free from the haughty style of European royalty and yet dignified enough to suit the head of a new government and his wife. Crowns were out. Bowing was in. (Hand-shaking came later, during Thomas Jefferson's administration.) Politics was not to be discussed in social settings. Events ended after the President and his wife left the room.

The Washingtons settled on a social calendar that included a gentlemen-only gathering on Tuesday afternoons (hosted by Washington alone) and a co-ed reception on Friday evenings (Martha and George hosted these together). Sundays were a day of rest from official duties. The couple established the tradition of a New Year's Day open house the first time this date came up on the presidential calendar. In addition to such planned events, Martha kept busy with the time-consuming practice of "calling" on other important wives. Since these women did the same thing, too, they often failed to find one another at home. Then custom required the disappointed visitor to leave behind a "calling card." The etiquette of the times expected the recipient of such cards to return the calls. With no telephones, Internet, or wireless service at one's disposal (not to mention no better transportation than horse and carriage), such a circuit easily became an exercise in exasperation. Nonetheless Martha tried to return all calls before three days had elapsed.

When George Washington left the Presidency after his second term (another precedent, and eventually, a law), he and Martha were finally free to settle for good at Mount Vernon. They returned happily to the pastoral setting, and they welcomed frequent visitors. Although Martha's children had both died by that time, they had grandchildren to enjoy. Then the former President died suddenly during the administration of his successor. Martha lived not even three years more than her husband.

Among the precedents Martha established as the widow of a President was to help shape the legacy of how her husband would be remembered. She burned their personal correspondence (to keep private the tenderness of their relationship), for example, and entertained patiently the dignitaries who came to pay their respects at Washington's grave. Such acts helped influence the reputation that outlived their lifetimes. The pair were buried beside one another, establishing one final tradition for future presidential couples to follow.

This miniature portrait (left page) dates from the early days of the American Revolution when Martha Washington was about 45 years old. About 12 years later she would become the first woman to take on the role of First Lady. Washington kept the tiny painting with him in a locket. She stood faithfully beside husband George Washington from the time of their marriage (above, left) through the final years of their life together (above, right).

Abigail Adams

THE JOHN ADAMS ADMINISTRATION ★ *1797 – 1801*

PRESIDENT	John Adams (1735–1826), 2nd President
MAIDEN NAME	Abigail Smith
BORN	Nov. 11, 1744, in Weymouth, Mass.
WEDDING	Oct. 25, 1764
AGE AT MARRIAGE	19 years old
THEIR CHILDREN	Abigail (1765), John Quincy (1767), Charles (1770), Thomas (1772)
AGE AS FIRST LADY	52 years old
DIED	Oct. 28, 1818, in Quincy, Mass.
AGE AT DEATH	73 years old
GRAVE	United First Parish Church, Quincy, Mass.

Did You Know?

• Abigail Adams is often quoted for advice she sent to her husband during the drafting of the Declaration of Independence. She wrote in 1776: "Remember the ladies and be more generous and favorable to them than your ancestors! Do not put unlimited power into the hands of husbands."

Later in life, Abigail Adams (above) felt it was more dignified to be painted with her head covered.

As FIRST LADY, ABIGAIL ADAMS STAYED TRUE to her character. Although she continued the social customs begun by her predecessor, she brought a more active and challenging mind to the job, too.

That lively wit was one of the qualities that had first attracted John Adams to his future bride, then 17. Abigail, the daughter of Congregational minister William Smith and his wife, Elizabeth Quincy Smith, wed the future President two years later. Their respect for one another as intellectual equals sustained their marriage forever after, often through the letters they exchanged during the long absences caused by Adams's government service.

With rare exception Abigail stayed home in Massachusetts while her husband traveled. She managed the family farm, marketed their crops, raised the couple's four children, and kept herself and her husband (via their correspondence) informed about local politics. "In all she appears [to have done] equally well," observed a grandson years later. She did join her husband during one of his foreign service tours in Europe, however. From 1784 to 1788 she lived abroad with Adams, first in France and then in England. Such experiences aided her later when she became First Lady.

Abigail was the first First Lady to live in the White House. Her tenure there was brief, since she first resided with her husband at the temporary nation's capital in Philadelphia. When she joined her husband in Washington, D.C., the executive mansion was still under construction, as indeed was most of the capital city itself.

The volumes of letters she exchanged with her husband and other key figures of the era remain a valuable record, not only of her personal relationships but also of the times themselves.

In 1800 Abigail Adams moved into the still incomplete White House. She grumbled in private about its inconveniences, but carefully instructed others to "say that I wrote you the situation is beautiful." Abigail earned praise for her beauty in youth (left page) and at maturity.

Martha Jefferson

THE JEFFERSON ADMINISTRATION ★ *1801 – 1809*

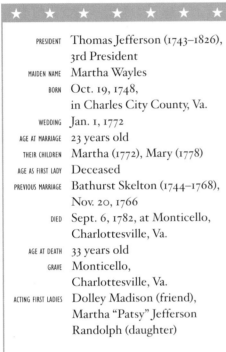

PRESIDENT	Thomas Jefferson (1743–1826), 3rd President
MAIDEN NAME	Martha Wayles
BORN	Oct. 19, 1748, in Charles City County, Va.
WEDDING	Jan. 1, 1772
AGE AT MARRIAGE	23 years old
THEIR CHILDREN	Martha (1772), Mary (1778)
AGE AS FIRST LADY	Deceased
PREVIOUS MARRIAGE	Bathurst Skelton (1744–1768), Nov. 20, 1766
DIED	Sept. 6, 1782, at Monticello, Charlottesville, Va.
AGE AT DEATH	33 years old
GRAVE	Monticello, Charlottesville, Va.
ACTING FIRST LADIES	Dolley Madison (friend), Martha "Patsy" Jefferson Randolph (daughter)

Did You Know?
• Before the development of birth control, the physical demands of frequent pregnancies shortened the lives of many women, including Martha Jefferson.

"In every scheme of happiness, she is placed in the foreground of the picture....
Take that away, and there is no picture for me."

— Thomas Jefferson, *1771, writing about his future wife*

As THE NATION'S THIRD PRESIDENT, Thomas Jefferson brought a previously unknown problem with him to the job: He lacked a wife. Whereas the nation's first two Presidents had wives to partner with them during their administrations, Jefferson did not. His one and only marriage had ended more than 18 years earlier with the death of his wife, Martha. Even though Martha Jefferson never actually served as First Lady, she is still accorded that honor in many history books in recognition of her standing as a President's wife.

Martha, like Jefferson, was born and raised in Virginia. She was the daughter of a planter and lawyer, John Wayles, and his wife Martha Eppes Wayles. Martha was a widow when she met the future President. Her first marriage had ended after two years with the death of her husband. Her son from this marriage would not survive either. Martha and Jefferson were wed soon after this boy's death. The newlyweds made do with temporary quarters while their future home of Monticello took shape nearby. They loved to perform together on harpsichord (Martha) and violin (Jefferson).

Over the ten years of their marriage, Martha gave birth to six children, but only three were alive when she died in 1782. Just two survived to adulthood. One of these, a daughter named for her mother but known as Patsy, acted as hostess during her father's administration. (Jefferson's other daughter, Mary, died during his Presidency.)

Dolley Madison, longtime friend of the President and wife of his Secretary of State, assisted as well. The social customs of the times required a woman to be present as hostess whenever women were among the invited guests. The aid of these women made it possible for President Jefferson to entertain properly.

The portrait shown (left page) is not of Thomas Jefferson's wife, Martha (of whom no likeness survives), but of his eldest daughter, also named Martha. After her father became President, this young woman would substitute regularly for her deceased mother as his hostess. Martha "Patsy" Jefferson Randolph gave birth to the first child at the White House, too, a son named in honor of James Madison.

Dolley Madison

THE MADISON ADMINISTRATION ★ *1809 – 1817*

PRESIDENT	James Madison (1751–1836), 4th President
MAIDEN NAME	Dolley Dandridge Payne
BORN	May 20, 1768, in Guilford County, N.C.
WEDDING	Sept. 15, 1794
AGE AT MARRIAGE	26 years old
THEIR CHILDREN	None
AGE AS FIRST LADY	40 years old
PREVIOUS MARRIAGE	John Todd (17??–1793),
AND CHILD	Jan. 7, 1790; John (1792)
DIED	July 12, 1849, in Washington, D.C.
AGE AT DEATH	81 years old
GRAVE	Montpelier, Orange County, Va.

Did You Know?

• Dolley Payne Todd was expelled from the Quaker Society of Friends when she wed James Madison, a non-Quaker.

In August 1814, near the end of the War of 1812, Dolley Madison packed up precious national treasures like the Declaration of Independence (above) as British forces advanced on the nation's capital. She fled from the White House with a wagon full of artifacts as her husband rallied U.S. troops.

DOLLEY MADISON WAS NO NEWCOMER to the White House social scene when her husband became the nation's fourth President. Already she had served Thomas Jefferson as a hostess. Even after her husband's Presidency, she endured as the grande dame of Washington, D.C., society. Dolley set standards for entertaining, advised younger First Ladies, and even introduced a President's son (Abraham Van Buren) to his bride.

As the daughter of John and Mary Coles Payne, who were merchants and former planters, Dolley was raised with the simple lifestyle of the Quaker faith. Her first marriage ended after only three years with the death of husband John Todd from yellow fever. Their son, John Payne Todd, survived. James Madison, still a bachelor at age 43, began courting her the following year, and the couple were soon married. She was 17 years younger than her new husband and several inches taller. She referred to him playfully as the "great little Madison" and called him by his last name throughout their marriage.

Dolley was the first First Lady to attend a husband's Inauguration. During the War of 1812, she gained lasting fame for spiriting valuable documents and furnishings out of the White House even as the sounds of battle could be heard in the distance. She insisted that the portrait of George Washington be cut from its frame (which was screwed to the wall) rather than leave it behind. When she and her husband returned to the White House, they found it burned and in ruins.

For the rest of Madison's Presidency, the couple lived elsewhere so the White House could be rebuilt. They moved into the nearby Octagon House, a home designed and built by the architect of the U.S. Capitol building.

Freed by her second marriage from the simple lifestyle of her childhood Quaker faith, Dolley Madison (left page) dressed and entertained lavishly. Dolley's political skills are credited with helping her husband win reelection during the War of 1812. After her husband's death in 1836, she relocated from their Virginia home to the nation's capital. "Mrs. Madison is the most brilliant hostess this country has ever known," claimed President Martin Van Buren. Sadly, reckless spending by her adult son complicated the finances of her retirement years.

Elizabeth Monroe

THE MONROE ADMINISTRATION ★ 1817 – 1825

Did You Know?

- The Monroes used French as their language of choice for family conversations.
- President Monroe and his First Lady hosted a dinner during 1824 with the Marquis de Lafayette and his wife as guests of honor, almost 30 years after Elizabeth had helped rescue Adrienne Lafayette from execution in France.
- Elizabeth Monroe may have suffered from epilepsy; she was badly burned near the end of her life after suffering a seizure beside a fireplace.

> "Mrs. Monroe is an elegant, accomplished woman. She possesses a charming mind and dignity of manners."
>
> — newspaper commentary, 1817

LIKE ALL OF THE EARLY FIRST LADIES, Elizabeth Monroe was born as a British subject. Her parents were Hannah Aspinwall Kortright and Lawrence Kortright, a British Army officer and successful New York City merchant. Her father remained neutral during the Revolutionary War. It appears that Elizabeth met her future husband while he was attending the 1785 session of the Continental Congress in New York. The two were married the next year.

Elizabeth is most remembered for the life she helped save during the French Revolution. She and James Monroe were stationed in Paris at the time, while her husband was serving as foreign minister for President George Washington. Marie-Adrienne Lafayette, the wife of Revolutionary War hero the Marquis de Lafayette, was imprisoned and at risk of being sent to the guillotine. Elizabeth made a dramatic visit to see her. Rather than risk offense to Elizabeth's husband (and, by extension, the U.S. government) revolutionary leaders ordered the release of their prisoner.

When Elizabeth reached the White House, she rejected one social custom. No longer would the First Lady return social calls. Although the move was received coolly at the time, other First Ladies were happy to follow her precedent.

Maria Monroe, the youngest of the Monroes' two daughters, was married during her father's first term of office. Although not the first White House wedding (that distinction falls to the Madison administration), it was the first one for a President's child.

"Though no longer young, she is still a very handsome woman," noted one White House guest in 1825 about First Lady Elizabeth Monroe (left page). Among her surviving possessions is a "French necessity kit" (above) for carrying small articles.

Louisa Adams

THE JOHN QUINCY ADAMS ADMINISTRATION ★ 1825 – 1829

PRESIDENT	John Quincy Adams (1767–1848), 6th President
MAIDEN NAME	Louisa Catherine Johnson
BORN	Feb. 12, 1775, in London, England
WEDDING	July 26, 1797
AGE AT MARRIAGE	22 years old
THEIR CHILDREN	George (1801), John (1803), Charles (1807)
AGE AS FIRST LADY	50 years old
DIED	May 14, 1852, in Washington, D.C.
AGE AT DEATH	77 years old
GRAVE	United First Parish Church, Quincy, Mass.

Did You Know?

• The second son of Louisa and John Quincy Adams was married in the White House in 1828. His bride was a niece of his mother's.

Two political rivals are pictured together in this illustration of a ball hosted by Louisa Adams. Her husband (at left) defeated Andrew Jackson (center) in the election of 1824.

LOUISA ADAMS, THE NATION'S ONLY foreign-born First Lady, met her future husband for the first time when she was living with her parents in France. She was four years old; John Quincy Adams was 12. Louisa's father, Joshua Johnson, was an American businessman living overseas with his British wife, Catherine Nuth Johnson. Louisa had been born at their home in London, England. Soon afterward, her family had moved to France for their safety during the American Revolution.

Some 15 years passed before the future President and First Lady crossed paths again. By then Louisa's family had returned to London, and her father was serving as a diplomat for the U.S. government. Louisa's first visit to the United States came in 1801 after she had married John Quincy Adams.

In 1809 her husband's own diplomatic career took them to Russia, where he served as U.S. minister during the Madison administration. In 1814 national business called him to western Europe. Soon he asked Louisa to join him. She traveled by carriage through winter weather for 40 days from St. Petersburg to meet him in Paris. Her chief traveling companion was their eight-year-old son, Charles. Two older sons, George and John, were already in school in the United States at the time. The Adamses' infant daughter had died the previous year.

Louisa, who preferred the city of Washington, D.C., over country life at the family homestead in Massachusetts, was nonetheless apprehensive when John Quincy Adams became President in 1825. Their one term in the White House was marred by persistent sniping between members of political parties and pointed criticism of her husband. Her own health concerns, including depression, became a problem, too.

The couple retired briefly from politics. John Quincy Adams returned to Washington as a U.S. Congressman in 1831. After his death in 1848, Louisa remained there.

Louisa Adams (left page) played the harp, composed music, and wrote poetry. Her husband called her a "faithful and affectionate wife, and a...tender, indulgent, and watchful mother."

THE AURA OF YOUTH

★ 1829 – 1861 ★

1830

Godey's Lady's Book *became the first U.S. women's magazine. Its editor, Sarah Josepha Hale, may be best remembered for writing the poem "Mary Had a Little Lamb."*

1833 – 1834

Prudence Crandall established a school in Connecticut for African-American girls. Her arrest, legal challenges, and violence eventually forced her to close the school.

1837

Mary Lyon founded Mount Holyoke Female Seminary in Massachusetts, the nation's first women's college. That same year formerly all-male Oberlin College of Ohio began admitting women.

1844

Margaret Fuller's Woman in the Nineteenth Century *helped fuel the demand for increased women's rights in the United States.*

Beginning in the 1820s a "Cult of Womanhood" developed that emphasized feminine qualities like youthful beauty, motherhood, and duty to husband and home. In the three decades prior to the Civil War, only three presidential wives, all young themselves, embraced the role of First Lady. Other spouses remained essentially absent, either because of death, illness, or reluctance to appear in the spotlight. Younger women, often their daughters or nieces, played the role of White House hostess in their stead. Deaths in office of two Presidents and a First Lady added to the period's lack of continuity.

1847

Self-taught astronomer Maria Mitchell, of Nantucket, Mass., discovered a comet. The next year she was honored as the first woman elected to the American Academy of Arts and Sciences.

1848

Advocates of increased rights for women issued a "Declaration of Rights and Sentiments" during a meeting in Seneca Falls, N.Y., that inaugurated women's quest for the right to vote.

1851

Amelia Bloomer sought to popularize the wearing of "the Turkish dress," or, as they came to be known, bloomers. Her attempt to reform women's fashions ended before the decade was out.

1854

Massachusetts joined the trend begun in 1848 by New York State and passed legislation granting women the right to own their own property, even if married.

Rachel Jackson

THE JACKSON ADMINISTRATION ★ *1829 – 1837*

★ ★ ★ ★ ★ ★ ★

PRESIDENT	Andrew Jackson (1767–1845), 7th President
MAIDEN NAME	Rachel Donelson
BORN	June 15?, 1767, in Halifax County, Va.
WEDDING	Aug. 1791 and Jan. 17, 1794
AGE AT MARRIAGE	24 years old
THEIR CHILDREN	None
AGE AS FIRST LADY	Deceased
PREVIOUS MARRIAGE	Lewis Robards (dates uncertain), March 1, 1785 (ended in divorce)
DIED	Dec. 22, 1828, at The Hermitage, Nashville, Tenn.
AGE AT DEATH	61 years old
GRAVE	The Hermitage, Nashville, Tenn.
ACTING FIRST LADIES	Emily Donelson (niece), Sarah Yorke Jackson (nephew's wife)

Did You Know?
• The Jacksons never had children of their own, but they helped raise members of their extended family.

Rachel's niece, Emily Donelson (above) served as First Lady until her death in 1836.

ALTHOUGH RACHEL JACKSON LIVED TO HEAR of her husband's election to the Presidency, she died from a heart attack before he could take office. Andrew Jackson blamed his political opponents for her death, knowing that she had been troubled by the slanderous remarks that fell on him—and on her—during his presidential campaign. Many critics focused on their distant past and the details of Rachel's two marriages. "Those vile wretches who have slandered her must look to God for mercy," Andrew Jackson is said to have remarked during her burial service.

Rachel's first marriage took place when she was 17 after she had grown up on the country's western frontier as the daughter of a surveyor. She was one of 11 children born to John and Rachel Stockley Donelson. Her marriage to Lewis Robards was troubled by his fits of jealousy, and twice she was separated from him. During the first interlude she met and fell in love with Andrew Jackson. When her husband filed for divorce in 1791, Rachel and Jackson were married. Not until 1794 did they learn that this divorce had never been granted, thus making their marriage illegal. Although the divorce later came through and they remarried, charges of bigamy, being married to two people at the same time, plagued Rachel from then on. Two nieces stood in for Rachel as First Lady.

Rachel Jackson (left page, in her youth) preferred to ride a saddled horse (as opposed to riding in a carriage) and liked to smoke a corncob pipe. She died ten weeks before her husband's Inauguration. The grieving Andrew Jackson slept nearby a tiny painted portrait of his wife and carried the little painting on his body each day, much as someone now might carry a snapshot in a wallet. The divorce decree from Rachel's first marriage is pictured above.

Hannah Van Buren

THE VAN BUREN ADMINISTRATION ★ *1837 – 1841*

PRESIDENT	Martin Van Buren (1782–1862), 8th President
MAIDEN NAME	Hannah Hoes
BORN	Mar. 8, 1783, in Kinderhook, N.Y.
WEDDING	Feb. 21, 1807
AGE AT MARRIAGE	23 years old
THEIR CHILDREN	Abraham (1807), John (1810), Martin (1812), Smith (1817)
AGE AS FIRST LADY	Deceased
DIED	Feb. 5, 1819, in Albany, N.Y.
AGE AT DEATH	35 years old
GRAVE	Kinderhook, N.Y.
ACTING FIRST LADY	Angelica Singleton Van Buren (daughter-in-law)

Did You Know?

• The Van Burens were born as U.S. citizens near the end of the Revolutionary War. They are the first presidential couple to not have lived at least part of their lives as subjects of the British crown.

Angelica Singleton (above) was introduced to her future husband Abraham Van Buren by her cousin, former First Lady Dolley Madison.

MARTIN VAN BUREN, LIKE HIS PREDECESSOR and mentor Andrew Jackson, came to the White House as a widower. His wife Hannah had died nearly 18 years earlier when she was only 35 years old.

Hannah, the daughter of Dutch-speaking John and Maria Quackenboss Hoes, grew up in the same New York State community as her future husband. The two were not only distant cousins but childhood sweethearts, as well. Martin fondly called his wife Jannetje, the Dutch version of Hannah. The two of them spoke Dutch at home, not English.

Little information was recorded about this wife of a future President. It is known that she was a faithful church member with the Dutch Reformed Church and later the Presbyterians. She gave birth to five sons in ten years, four of whom lived into adulthood. Hannah became ill when her youngest son was still an infant. Soon after he turned two, she died from tuberculosis, at that time a fatal lung disease. Her gravestone pays tribute to her as "a sincere Christian, a dutiful child, tender mother, affectionate wife."

Hannah's death ended the Van Buren marriage after only 11 years. Even though Van Buren was only 36 years old, he never remarried. At the time of his election in 1836, none of his sons were married either. All four bachelors moved into the White House with their father.

His eldest son Abraham married some 18 months later. Abraham served as secretary to his father, and his new wife, Angelica Singleton Van Buren, became the hostess of the White House. Angelica was the daughter of prosperous South Carolina plantation (and slave) owners. Her Southern heritage helped balance the Northern background of the President's family at a time of growing tension between these two regions over the use of slave labor in the South.

A gold brooch bears this likeness of Hannah Hoes Van Buren (left page). Angelica Singleton Van Buren, who married Hannah's eldest son during the second year of Martin Van Buren's administration, served as First Lady in the place of her deceased mother-in-law.

Anna Harrison

THE WILLIAM HENRY HARRISON ADMINISTRATION ★ *1841*

★ ★ ★ ★ ★ ★ ★

PRESIDENT	William Henry Harrison (1773–1841), 9th President
MAIDEN NAME	Anna Tuthill Symmes
BORN	July 25, 1775, in Morristown, N.J.
WEDDING	Nov. 25, 1795
AGE AT MARRIAGE	20 years old
THEIR CHILDREN	Elizabeth (1796), John Cleves (1798), Lucy (1800), William (1802), John Scott (1804), Benjamin (1806), Mary (1809), Carter (1811), Anna (1813)
AGE AS FIRST LADY	65 years old
DIED	Feb. 25, 1864, in North Bend, Ohio
AGE AT DEATH	88 years old
GRAVE	Harrison Tomb State Memorial, North Bend, Ohio
ACTING FIRST LADY	Jane Irwin Harrison (daughter-in-law)

Did You Know?

• Anna Harrison was the first First Lady to be educated outside of the home on a regular basis. She attended two schools in the New York City area, including a boarding school located on Broadway in lower Manhattan.

• Soon after her husband's death, Congress awarded Anna the first presidential widow's pension, a stipend of $25,000 that equaled the Chief Executive's salary.

• John Scott, the only Harrison child to outlive his parents, was himself the father of future President Benjamin Harrison.

• Anna died at age 88, outliving her husband by 22 years.

• Anna was the first of five First Ladies to be buried in Ohio. Only New York State (with six First Lady graves) and Virginia (with eight) may claim to serve as the resting place for more presidential wives.

WHEN ANNA HARRISON AND HER HUSBAND parted in early 1841 so he could travel east for his Inauguration, the couple expected to be reunited later that year in Washington, D.C. Anna planned to make the difficult journey from their home in Ohio after winter weather ended. Instead William Henry Harrison died shortly after taking office, making his Presidency the shortest on record and preventing his wife from serving as First Lady. Had their plans worked out, the nation's second oldest President would have introduced the nation's oldest First Lady, at age 65, to the White House.

Anna was the daughter of John Cleves Symmes, a judge, and Anna Tuthill Symmes. She met her future husband as a young woman while traveling with her father to the western frontier. The pair were married secretly soon after. From then on she and William made their homes variously at frontier forts (where he served as an Army officer), in the nation's capital (during his service in Congress), and at the fledgling government seat for the Indiana Territory (where he was governor).

She bore nine children, making her the mother of more children than any other President's wife. She outlived all but one of them.

Knowing his wife's arrival in the nation's capital would be delayed, President-elect Harrison had recruited his daughter-in-law to serve temporarily in Anna's place. Jane Irwin Harrison, whose own husband had died three years earlier, thus served as First Lady for this briefest of presidential administrations.

This portrait of Anna Harrison (left page) was painted when she was in her late 60s, two years after the death of her husband, President William Henry Harrison. She is still dressed in the traditional mourning color of black. Her daughter-in-law Jane Irwin Harrison (above), served in her place as First Lady during the nation's shortest Presidency.

Letitia Tyler

THE TYLER ADMINISTRATION ★ *1841 – 1845*

★ ★ ★ ★ ★ ★ ★

PRESIDENT	John Tyler (1790–1862), 10th President
MAIDEN NAME	Letitia Christian
BORN	Nov. 12, 1790, in New Kent County, Va.
WEDDING	Mar. 29, 1813
AGE AT MARRIAGE	22 years old
THEIR CHILDREN	Mary (1815), Robert (1816), John (1819), Letitia (1821), Elizabeth (1823), Alice (1827), Tazewell (1830)
AGE AS FIRST LADY	50 years old
DIED	Sept. 10, 1842, in Washington, D.C.
AGE AT DEATH	51 years old
GRAVE	Cedar Grove, Va.
ACTING FIRST LADIES	Priscilla Cooper Tyler (daughter-in-law), Letitia Tyler Semple (daughter)
PRESIDENT'S OTHER WIVES	*see next page*
OTHER CHILDREN	*see next page*

Did You Know?

- Customs of the times led to a lengthy courtship (five years) for John and Letitia Tyler, a delayed first kiss (only weeks before their wedding), and its placement on an innocent spot (her hand).
- Because of ill health, Letitia Tyler attended only one official function at the White House, the wedding of daughter Elizabeth in January 1842.
- Letitia Tyler was the first First Lady to die during a Presidency. A stroke ended her life during the second year of her husband's term of office.
- The seven surviving children born to Letitia Tyler made up half of the total number fathered by John Tyler. His second wife (see next page) bore him another seven children, making him the father of more children than any other President.

LETITIA TYLER CAME TO THE WHITE HOUSE an invalid, having been partially paralyzed by a stroke two years before her husband became President. She became the first First Lady to die during a Presidency when a second stroke claimed her life early in John Tyler's administration. Her death at age 51 made her the youngest presidential wife to die during or after a Presidency. (A few wives died at younger ages, but their deaths occurred long before their husbands became President.)

Letitia, the daughter of Robert and Mary Brown Christian, grew up on a Virginia plantation staffed with slave labor. She and the future President, also a Virginian, courted for five years before marrying. Letitia gave birth to seven children in 15 years who survived to adulthood. An eighth child died young.

Tyler's Presidency began with the death in office of William Henry Harrison. He was the first Vice President to succeed a deceased President. First Lady Letitia Tyler confined herself to the White House family quarters and directed the affairs of the mansion from there. Her new daughter-in-law, Priscilla Cooper Tyler, took over as official White House hostess. Priscilla noted that "mother attends to and regulates all the household affairs and all so quietly that you can't tell when she does it."

In 1844 Priscilla and her husband moved to Philadelphia. Letitia Tyler Semple served briefly as First Lady until the surprise marriage of her father and Julia Gardiner later that year.

This portrait of Letitia Tyler (left page) was painted before she suffered a crippling stroke in her late 40s. Upon arriving at the White House two years later, she passed the hostess duties of the First Lady to her daughter-in-law, Priscilla Cooper. John Tyler hosted this party for children (above) at the White House.

Julia Tyler

THE TYLER ADMINISTRATION ★ *1841 – 1845*

PRESIDENT	John Tyler (1790–1862), 10th President
MAIDEN NAME	Julia Gardiner
BORN	May 4, 1820, in Gardiners Island, N.Y.
WEDDING	June 26, 1844
AGE AT MARRIAGE	24 years old
THEIR CHILDREN	David (1846), John Alexander (1848), Julia (1849), Lachlan (1851), Lyon (1853), Robert (1856), Pearl (1860)
AGE AS FIRST LADY	24 years old
DIED	July 10, 1889, in Richmond, Va.
AGE AT DEATH	69 years old
GRAVE	Hollywood Cemetery, Richmond, Va.
PRESIDENT'S OTHER WIVES	*see previous page*
OTHER CHILDREN	*see previous page*

Did You Know?

• Julia Tyler, when widowed in 1862, was left with seven children to raise between the ages of 18 months and 15 years.
• Julia's death took place at the same hotel and in the same room where her husband had himself died decades earlier.

> **"After I lost my father, I felt differently toward the President. He seemed... to be more agreeable...than any younger man."**
>
> — Julia Tyler

THE SECRET COURTSHIP OF JULIA GARDINER and President John Tyler grew out of a period of personal loss for both individuals. Tyler's first wife, Letitia, had died during his Presidency 17 months earlier, and Julia's father, state senator David Gardiner, had recently been killed in a gun explosion during a Potomac River cruise attended by both the President and his future First Lady. John Tyler and Julia had first met some months before Letitia's death and had begun courting soon after it. They became engaged soon after her father's accidental death.

The couple were married four months later at a private ceremony in New York City not far from the bride's Long Island birthplace. Two of Julia's siblings attended the wedding, as may have her mother, Juliana McLachlan Gardiner. Only one Tyler child, John, knew in advance of the wedding and attended. He was about one year younger than his stepmother.

At 24 Julia Tyler became the youngest First Lady to that point, and the second youngest ever, topped only by Grover Cleveland's White House bride, Frances. Julia and John Tyler hold the record for the greatest age difference between a President and his First Lady, 30 years.

Julia's brief tenure as First Lady lasted for the final eight months of her husband's Presidency. Then the pair retired to a plantation in Virginia that became home to their five sons and two daughters. These offspring, combined with the seven surviving children of his first marriage, make John Tyler the father of more children than any other President.

Although painted three years after her service as First Lady, this portrait (left page) still captures the youthful beauty that Julia Tyler brought to the White House near the end of John Tyler's administration. Widowed at age 41, Julia (above) never remarried.

Sarah Polk

THE POLK ADMINISTRATION ★ *1845 – 1849*

PRESIDENT	James K. Polk (1795–1849), 11th President
MAIDEN NAME	Sarah Childress
BORN	Sept. 4, 1803, in Murfreesboro, Tenn.
WEDDING	Jan. 1, 1824
AGE AT MARRIAGE	20 years old
THEIR CHILDREN	None
AGE AS FIRST LADY	41 years old
SPECIAL INTERESTS	Served as President's personal secretary
DIED	Aug. 14, 1891, in Nashville, Tenn.
AGE AT DEATH	87 years old
GRAVE	State Capitol Grounds, Nashville, Tenn.

Did You Know?

• Sarah Polk spent almost twice as long mourning the death of her husband as the couple had spent in marriage.

• Sarah lived with such grace at their Nashville home that Polk Place was viewed as neutral ground during the Civil War.

Later in life Sarah Polk adopted a great niece. This photo (above) was taken during a visit the pair made to the Hermitage, President Andrew Jackson's Tennessee home.

SARAH POLK'S TENURE AS FIRST LADY followed a series of administrations where youthful stand-ins had shouldered most of the responsibilities of White House hostess. Sarah sought no such assistance and approached her job with an expanded view of its scope.

The daughter of successful planter Joel Childress and his wife, Elizabeth Whitsitt Childress, Sarah met her future husband when they studied with the same teacher. Better educated than the average girl of that era, Sarah married James K. Polk some eight years later while he was serving in the Tennessee House of Representatives. Their 25-year marriage produced no children, leaving Sarah free to become more involved in her husband's career than most wives of the time.

Unlike many other political wives, Sarah lived with her husband in Washington, D.C., after he became a member of the U.S. Congress. She screened his professional reading, offered political advice, built networks of her own among Washington insiders, and even helped draft his speeches.

After her husband became President, Sarah continued such efforts and met the social responsibilities of being First Lady as well. Dancing was downplayed because of her religious beliefs. She preferred to entertain with gracious, informed conversation and fine dining. The first White House Thanksgiving dinner was held under her direction. She introduced gas lights, too. (Candles had sufficed before.)

The Polks enjoyed the briefest of any shared presidential retirement. James K. Polk died just 103 days after leaving office. Sarah went on to live 42 more years, outliving her husband by a greater span of time than any other First Lady. For the rest of her life she wore the mourning color of black.

This portrait (left page) copies one made of Sarah Polk during her husband's Presidency. Sarah came to the White House as one of the nation's youngest First Ladies, only 41 years of age. Her youth, combined with the couple's childless household, left her with the time and energy to maintain a close involvement in her husband's administration. Polk, whose own health was more frail than hers, relied on her for secretarial work as well as advice.

Margaret Taylor

PRESIDENT	Zachary Taylor (1784–1850), 12th President
MAIDEN NAME	Margaret Mackall Smith
BORN	Sept. 21, 1788, in Calvert County, Md.
WEDDING	June 21, 1810
AGE AT MARRIAGE	21 years old
THEIR CHILDREN	Ann (1811), Sarah (1814), Mary (1824), Richard (1826)
AGE AS FIRST LADY	60 years old
DIED	Aug. 18, 1852, in Pascagoula, Miss.
AGE AT DEATH	63 years old
GRAVE	Zachary Taylor National Cemetery, Louisville, Ky.
ACTING FIRST LADY	Mary Elizabeth Taylor Bliss (daughter)

Did You Know?

- The Taylors' daughter Sarah eloped to marry future Confederacy president Jefferson Davis; she died from malaria three months later.
- Margaret Taylor inherited five slaves from her husband. She was one of a number of First Ladies, from Martha Washington to Ellen Arthur, whose families relied upon slave labor during their childhoods, as adults, or both.

Mary Elizabeth "Betty" Taylor Bliss (above) took over the official duties of First Lady for her mother, who declined the role.

MARGARET "PEGGY" TAYLOR RESUMED the pattern interrupted by Sarah Polk of delegating the duties of First Lady to a younger family member. This trend may have been fueled by the popularity at that time of youth and beauty. It may also have allowed Presidents' wives to escape the risk of social criticism. Many of the First Ladies from the middle decades of the 19th century had not enjoyed the same experiences as the earliest wives of Presidents. Few had traveled abroad, for example, or been entertained at royal courts.

Prior to her husband's unexpected nomination for the Presidency, Peggy Taylor had anticipated retirement with her career-soldier husband on their Southern plantation. During the election campaign, she is said to have prayed for Zachary Taylor's defeat. When her prayers went unanswered, she moved into the second floor of the White House and generally remained there. Excuses for her isolation included poor health and an earlier pledge to give up social gatherings if her husband came home safely from the Mexican War (which he did).

Peggy had grown up on a Maryland plantation, the daughter of Walter and Ann Mackall Smith. She met Taylor during a visit to Kentucky, and they were married a year later. Peggy gave birth to five girls and one boy in the next 16 years, often shadowing the moves of her husband from one military outpost to the next. Two of their daughters died young.

Their youngest surviving daughter, Mary Elizabeth, took on the role of First Lady for her mother. Recently married, the young "Betty" Bliss hosted official functions with "the artlessness of a rustic belle and the grace of a duchess," according to one visitor. Peggy Taylor was content to mingle with family and friends in the private quarters of the Executive Mansion. Her daughter's reign as First Lady ended with the President's death.

Scholars debate whether or not an authentic likeness has survived of Margaret Taylor, but the image at left is suggested as a possible portrait. An acquaintance described her as "a most kind and thorough-bred Southern lady."

Abigail Fillmore

THE FILLMORE ADMINISTRATION ★ *1850 – 1853*

PRESIDENT	Millard Fillmore (1800–1874), 13th President
MAIDEN NAME	Abigail Powers
BORN	Mar. 13, 1798, in Stillwater, N.Y.
WEDDING	Feb. 5, 1826
AGE AT MARRIAGE	27 years old
THEIR CHILDREN	Millard (1828), Mary (1832)
AGE AS FIRST LADY	52 years old
EARLIER CAREER	Schoolteacher
SPECIAL INTEREST	White House library
DIED	Mar. 30, 1853, in Washington, D.C.
AGE AT DEATH	55 years old
GRAVE	Forest Lawn Cemetery, Buffalo, N.Y.
ASSISTING FIRST LADY	Mary Abigail Fillmore (daughter)
PRESIDENT'S OTHER WIVES	Caroline Carmichael McIntosh (1813–1881), second wife (married Feb. 10, 1858)
OTHER CHILDREN	None

Did You Know?

- Abigail Fillmore, at 5 feet 6 inches, was tall for a 19th-century woman but still considerably shorter than her 6-foot-tall husband.
- Abigail's mother and brother did not initially approve of her courtship by Millard Fillmore, the simple farm boy who went on to become President.
- Abigail played the piano and harp, and she added these instruments to the White House library she created. Abigail used the library as a place to entertain friends, perform with her daughter (who sang), and—of course—read a favorite book.
- Millard Fillmore became the first former President to remarry when he was wed to Caroline Carmichael McIntosh, herself a widow, five years after Abigail's death.

ABIGAIL FILLMORE, THE FIRST FIRST LADY TO have worked outside of the home, met her future husband on the job. She was a new schoolteacher, and he was her pupil. It was Millard Fillmore's first time in a classroom, and he gained not only an education from the experience but also a wife. After marrying, Abigail kept her job (another First Lady first) until she had children.

Abigail's father, a Baptist minister named Lemuel Powers, died soon after his daughter's birth. Her mother, Abigail Newland Powers, raised her daughter and a son on New York State's frontier. Abigail grew up with a love of reading. After they were married, Fillmore made a habit of returning home from business trips with a new book for his wife. The couple maintained a shared interest in politics, too. A mutual friend noted that Fillmore "never took any important step without [his wife's] counsel and advice."

When Fillmore's political career—and the death of Zachary Taylor—brought his family to the White House, Abigail continued the tradition of appointing a young First Lady assistant. Her teenage daughter, Mary Abigail, or "Abby," served as hostess on many occasions. Although the President's wife played that role herself at other times, Abigail preferred to work on a project she had taken on with the aid of $2,000 from the U.S. Congress: the creation of a White House library.

Abigail Fillmore earned the unfortunate distinction of having the shortest retirement of any First Lady. She caught a cold after attending the snowy Inauguration of her husband's successor. She developed pneumonia and died before the month was out.

Abigail Fillmore (left page) had a lifelong love of literature that led her to start a library at the White House (above, today). Before then all books were moved in and out with other personal property for each Presidency. Abigail's new library featured several hundred works of fiction, law, history, religion, and geography. She entertained a number of popular authors, too, including Charles Dickens and Washington Irving.

Jane Pierce

THE PIERCE ADMINISTRATION ★ *1853 – 1857*

PRESIDENT	Franklin Pierce (1804–1869), 14th President
MAIDEN NAME	Jane Means Appleton
BORN	Mar. 12, 1806, in Hampton, N.J.
WEDDING	Nov. 10, 1834
AGE AT MARRIAGE	28 years old
THEIR CHILDREN	Frank (1839), Benjamin (1841), both died young
AGE AS FIRST LADY	46 years old
DIED	Dec. 2, 1863, in Andover, Mass.
AGE AT DEATH	57 years old
GRAVE	Old North Cemetery, Concord, N.H.
ASSISTING FIRST LADIES	Abigail Kent Means (friend and aunt of First Lady), Varina Davis (friend of First Lady)

Did You Know?

• During her lifetime Jane Pierce survived the deaths of 14 close relatives, including her parents, two brothers (the first one died when she herself was just 11), a pregnant sister, and all of her own children. Her husband's death followed hers by six years.

Jane Pierce and her son Benjamin were captured in this photograph three years before his death in 1853.

UNHAPPINESS DOGGED THE STEPS OF Jane Pierce for much of her life. Her father Jesse Appleton, a Congregational minister and onetime president of Bowdoin College, died during her childhood. After Jane met Bowdoin graduate Franklin Pierce, her mother, Elizabeth Means Appleton, objected to their marriage. Pierce, after all, was a Democrat, and their family was not. (They married anyway.)

Although the couple began their marriage happily enough, Pierce's political career choice placed a growing strain on their union. Jane blamed the lifestyle of a politician with causing her husband to drink too much, and she disliked living in Washington, D.C. It is said that she fainted upon hearing the news of her husband's presidential nomination and later prayed regularly for his defeat.

Family tragedy struck between Pierce's victory and his Inauguration. Having already lost two of their three sons, their surviving son Benjamin died, too. He was killed in a train car derailment in January 1853. His parents, who witnessed the accident, were devastated. Jane viewed the tragedy as a judgment from God against her husband's devotion to politics. Her grief prevented her from attending the Inauguration. Although she moved into the White House, she withdrew from social functions for most of the first two years of her husband's administration. Not until New Year's Day of 1855 did she make a formal appearance, and even after that time her participation was irregular.

Abigail Kent Means, a childhood friend and aunt by marriage, stood in for her as hostess during these lapses. Varina Davis, another friend and the wife of Cabinet member (and future Confederacy president) Jefferson Davis, assisted as well.

Experience with death became a recurring theme for Jane Pierce (left page). In order to comply with the customs of the day, Jane spent some 17 years of her life in mourning, including at least one year each for the deaths of her parents and three sons. Mourners avoided parties, wore black clothes, and, if female, often veiled their faces.

Harriet Lane

THE BUCHANAN ADMINISTRATION ★ *1857 – 1861*

PRESIDENT	James Buchanan (1791–1868), 15th President
ACTING FIRST LADY	Harriet Lane (niece)
BORN	May 9, 1830, in Mercersburg, Pa.
AGE AS FIRST LADY	26 years old
MARRIAGE AND CHILDREN	Henry Elliott Johnston (18??–1884), Jan. 11, 1866; James (1866), Henry (1869)
DIED	July 3, 1903, in Rhode Island
AGE AT DEATH	73 years old
GRAVE	Green Mount Cemetery, Baltimore, Md.

Did You Know?

• Harriet Lane's private art collection became the basis for the Smithsonian Institution's National Collection of Fine Arts following her donation of it to the federal government.

• Johns Hopkins Hospital in Baltimore founded the Harriet Lane Outpatient Clinics using a bequest made by the former First Lady following her death. The clinic continues to care for young people today.

"I have lost the only earthly object of my affections.... My happiness will be buried with her."

— James Buchanan,
upon the death of his former fiancée Anne Coleman

ONLY ONE PRESIDENT NEVER MARRIED—James Buchanan. Although he brought no wife with him to the White House, he still needed someone to help plan and host the social events that came with his job. He delegated these tasks to his niece, Harriet Lane, a young woman whom he had helped raise following the deaths of her parents. (Her mother had been Buchanan's sister.) The 26-year-old Harriet, herself unmarried, moved into the White House with her uncle and went to work.

Harriet, who had traveled with Buchanan during his years of foreign service, brought royal court experience—and style—with her to the White House. (She had become acquainted with Queen Victoria, for example, during her uncle's diplomatic service in Great Britain.) As First Lady, Harriet restored a festive air to the Executive Mansion that had not been seen in decades. She maintained a sense of civility in social gatherings that was particularly to her credit given the looming threat of civil war. She started fashion trends (necklines dropped) and inspired songwriters (one dedicated "Listen to the Mockingbird" to her).

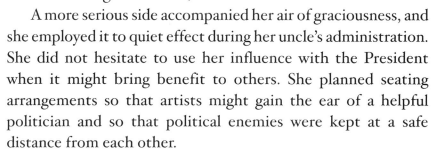

A more serious side accompanied her air of graciousness, and she employed it to quiet effect during her uncle's administration. She did not hesitate to use her influence with the President when it might bring benefit to others. She planned seating arrangements so that artists might gain the ear of a helpful politician and so that political enemies were kept at a safe distance from each other.

Harriet Lane (left page and above, in later years) served as First Lady for the nation's only bachelor President. She finally married years later at age 35. Sadly both her husband and their two sons died in the two following decades. As First Lady, Harriet's charm provided welcome relief from the growing threat of the Civil War.

EMERGING POLITICAL PARTNERS

★ *1861 – 1901* ★

1866

Elizabeth Cady Stanton of New York State became the first woman to run for Congress. She earned 24 votes.

1872

Victoria Claflin Woodhull became the first female candidate for President of the United States.

1873

The inventions of the typewriter in 1873 and the telephone three years later brought swelling numbers of women into the office workforce.

1879

Frances Willard became head of the Women's Christian Temperance Union and led a national campaign to ban the sale of alcohol. The 18th Amendment did just that from 1920 to 1933.

By mid-century, politics began to emerge as a lifelong career, and the role of a politician's wife evolved into one of supporting partnership. First Ladies acted more boldly to set the social customs and tone of the White House. The spread of mass media increased public interest in the lives of the Presidents and their families. Although full-fledged campaigning had yet to begin, wives played an increasing role in the political fortunes of their husbands. The Presidency made widows out of three First Ladies during this period when assassins killed their husbands.

1889

With the establishment of Hull-House in Chicago, Jane Addams helped create the settlement house movement to meet the needs of the nation's growing population of immigrants and their children.

1892

Ida B. Wells exposed the horrors and injustice of racism with a series of articles about the lynching of African Americans in the South.

1893

Colorado became the first state to offer women the right to vote in statewide elections since New Jersey closed its polls to women in 1807.

1896

Women's rights advocate Susan B. Anthony declared that riding bicycles "has done more to emancipate women than any one thing in the world" by giving "a feeling of self-reliance and independence."

Mary Todd Lincoln

THE LINCOLN ADMINISTRATION ★ 1861 – 1865

★ ★ ★ ★ ★ ★ ★

PRESIDENT Abraham Lincoln (1809–1865), 16th President

MAIDEN NAME Mary Todd

BORN Dec. 13, 1818, in Lexington, Ky.

WEDDING Nov. 4, 1842

AGE AT MARRIAGE 23 years old

THEIR CHILDREN Robert (1843), William (1850), Thomas (1853)

AGE AS FIRST LADY 42 years old

DIED July 16, 1882, in Springfield, Ill.

AGE AT DEATH 63 years old

GRAVE Oak Ridge Cemetery, Springfield, Ill.

Did You Know?

• Four of Mary Todd Lincoln's brothers and half-brothers fought on the Confederate side of the Civil War. Two died in the conflict.

Mary Todd Lincoln (above), at five feet, two inches in height, would have been dwarfed by her husband, Abraham Lincoln, the nation's tallest President at six feet, four inches.

FIRST LADIES ARE NO STRANGERS TO HARDSHIP, but few of them can match the personal tragedy and loss experienced by the wife of the nation's 16th President. Mary Todd Lincoln's husband died tragically, and all but one of her children did, too. At one point she was labeled insane and housed in an institution. Late in life she was nearly blind and partially paralyzed.

No one would have predicted such a sad ending would come for this bubbly daughter of a prosperous banker, Robert Smith Todd, and his wife Eliza Ann Parker Todd. Young Mary lived in comfort and received the best education then available to girls. Her training included French tutors, dance lessons, and boarding school. One tragedy befell her childhood—the death of her mother when she was six years old. Her father promptly remarried. Between his two wives he produced 15 children.

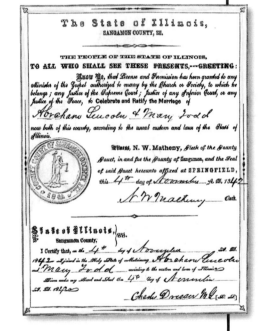

Mary may have developed her outgoing, flamboyant style to gain parental attention in this large blended family. Her habit of spending money as a form of comfort probably dates to this period, too. Perhaps buying new things helped Mary make up for the loss of her mother.

When she was 21, Mary went to live with her older sister in Springfield, Illinois. Soon afterward she met her future husband at a dance party. Their courtship moved slowly, but eventually

---

In 1842 Mary Todd and Abraham Lincoln were wed in Springfield, Illinois (above, their marriage license), at the home of Mary's sister. Mary Todd Lincoln (left page) was the first President's wife to be described in newspapers as "First Lady" of the land, although the term had been used to describe Harriet Lane in the previous administration.

"Did ever woman have to suffer so much and experience so great a change?"

— Mary Todd Lincoln, *following the assassination of Abraham Lincoln*

she and Abraham Lincoln were wed. The early years of their marriage were generally happy, marred only by the death of the second-born of their four sons. Three-year-old "Eddie" died of tuberculosis at a time when the absence of antibiotics and hospitals made such losses quite common.

Even before their marriage, Lincoln had begun to combine his legal experience with a career in politics. Mary was pleased, and she coveted the honor of President for her husband (and First Lady for herself) long before others might have considered such a goal to be reasonable. When her dream came true, she approached the role of White House hostess with an enthusiasm often missing from recent presidential spouses. Here, however, her story starts to go sour.

Perhaps no one could have been expected to manage the social obligations for a nation engaged in civil war. This challenge hampered Mary's efforts from the get-go. For starters, she was suspect because she had grown up in a state bordering the Confederacy. The fact that several of her brothers were fighting for the Southern cause did not help either. These topics became part of an avalanche of bad press that dogged the First Lady almost from the moment she reached Washington, D.C. Such media attention grew out of the controversy of the Civil War and an expanding interest among readers in gossipy, social news.

It seemed that nothing Mary did was right. When she dressed in stylish clothes, she was attacked for spending more money than was appropriate during wartime. When she wore plainer attire, her appearance was criticized. She earned equal condemnation whether she entertained lavishly or modestly. Her reluctance to let her oldest son fight in the war drew criticism. So did her formula for curing the blues: shopping. Mary bought compulsively, buying hundreds of pairs of gloves, for example, and spending beyond her means. Her mounting debt became just one more stress.

One of the Lincoln's three surviving sons—the middle boy, "Willie"—died suddenly in early 1862, probably from pneumonia. He was the only presidential child to die in the White House. The boy was just 11 years old, and both Lincolns were devastated. Mary grieved long and hard. This action, like just about everything else she did, drew criticism, too. How could her grief match the sorrow of families losing sons on the Civil War battlefields?

Mary's mental health was still fragile three years later when she faced the even greater shock of her husband's assassination. One moment Mary and Abraham were holding hands at a theater performance, the next minute he was mortally wounded. The timing of his death seemed especially cruel, coming just as the Civil War had ended and things were looking up for the nation and its First Family.

The bad fortune of Mary Todd Lincoln did not stop there. In debt and hounded by continuing negative press, she fled to Europe with her youngest son, "Tad." Although she found some peace there (and gained news of a Congressional pension that would relieve some of her financial woes), she returned home with an ill son. Tad soon died at just 18 years of age. Mary's mental health then deteriorated to the point where her only remaining son arranged to have her declared legally insane and placed in an institution (more to prevent her from spending his inheritance than for her own good). Such a pronouncement was like a death sentence for women of that era because it stripped them of all rights to property and made it difficult to seek the help of an attorney.

To her credit, Mary regained her equilibrium and engineered her release about four months later. She eventually was legally cleared of being insane, too. Both results were remarkable feats for that time. Her subsequent return to Europe brought the final tragedy, a bad fall that left her semi-paralyzed. Her sight was failing, too, triggered by health issues and, some said, from the irritation of extended periods of weeping.

Mary spent the final years of her life in seclusion at her sister's home in Springfield. Thus Mary Todd Lincoln came full circle, returning to the community where she first met her husband and the house where the two had been married so many years before. Her death followed his by 17 years. Her funeral included the minister's observation that the "bullet that sped its way and took her husband from earth took her too."

Happy moments in the life of Mary Todd Lincoln, such as hosting receptions at the White House with her husband (left page), were easily obscured by darker days, especially her husband's assassination (above, Mary weeps at his deathbed). Mary endured so much public criticism that she felt as "if I had committed murder in every state in this blessed Union." A staff member routinely screened her incoming letters in order to remove hate mail.

Eliza Johnson

THE ANDREW JOHNSON ADMINISTRATION ★ 1865 – 1869

PRESIDENT	Andrew Johnson (1808–1875), 17th President
MAIDEN NAME	Eliza McCardle
BORN	Oct. 4, 1810, in Leesburg, Tenn.
WEDDING	May 17, 1827
AGE AT MARRIAGE	16 years old
THEIR CHILDREN	Martha (1828), Charles (1830), Mary (1832), Robert (1834), Andrew (1852)
AGE AS FIRST LADY	54 years old
DIED	Jan. 15, 1876, in Green County, Tenn.
AGE AT DEATH	65 years old
GRAVE	Andrew Johnson National Historical Site, Greenville, Tenn.
ASSISTING FIRST LADY	Martha Johnson Patterson (daughter)

Did You Know?
• Eliza Johnson was better educated than her new husband and taught him how to write his letters and do arithmetic.

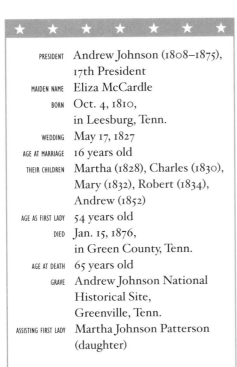

Souvenir hunters left the White House so damaged following Abraham Lincoln's assassination that Congress appropriated funds for its redecoration. Martha Johnson Patterson (above) supervised the work for her mother.

"WE ARE PLAIN PEOPLE, FROM THE MOUNTAINS of Tennessee," observed Martha Johnson Patterson after Abraham Lincoln's death made her father President. "I trust too much will not be expected of us."

Martha's mother Eliza was the daughter of a shoemaker, John McCardle and his wife, Sarah Phillips McCardle. Her father died during her childhood. She became the youngest bride of a future President when, at 16, she married a newcomer to town. Andrew Johnson, just 18 years old, was the youngest groom to later become President. Eliza raised their five children amidst the challenges of an often-absent husband (because of his political career) and the unfolding tensions of the Civil War. She lost both a son and a son-in-law during the conflict.

Eliza had only visited Washington, D.C., one time before her husband became President, and she had no interest in playing the role of White House hostess. She was so invisible (attending perhaps three events) that one newspaper suggested her existence was "almost a myth." Following earlier traditions, she entrusted her eldest daughter Martha with the social responsibilities of First Lady. Eliza preferred to manage the household from her private quarters, and she assisted her husband by screening important newspaper articles for him. The last of the reclusive First Ladies, Eliza added one more entry in the record books by dying just 168 days after her husband did, the narrowest gap between the deaths of any presidential spouses.

Eliza Johnson (left page) did not pose for this portrait. Instead the artist based his painting on a photograph that had been taken of the First Lady during her years in the White House. Eliza's daughter, Martha Johnson Patterson, handled hostess duties for her mother during her father's Presidency. The women persevered with their routines during the unprecedented impeachment trial of the President (above). They were confident he would be acquitted—and he was.

Julia Grant

THE GRANT ADMINISTRATION ★ *1869 – 1877*

PRESIDENT	Ulysses S. Grant (1822–1885), 18th President
MAIDEN NAME	Julia Boggs Dent
BORN	Jan. 26, 1826, in St. Louis, Mo.
WEDDING	Aug. 22, 1848
AGE AT MARRIAGE	22 years old
THEIR CHILDREN	Frederick (1850), Ulysses (1852), Ellen (1855), Jesse (1858)
AGE AS FIRST LADY	43 years old
DIED	Dec. 14, 1902, in Washington, D.C.
AGE AT DEATH	76 years old
GRAVE	General Grant National Memorial, New York, N.Y.

Did You Know?

• Julia Grant's father, a slave owner in Missouri, supported the Southern cause during the Civil War and broke off communication with his wife's husband during the conflict.

• Julia Grant was the first two-term First Lady in 44 years (since Elizabeth Monroe) because only one intervening President—widower Andrew Jackson—won reelection and lived to serve two complete terms in office.

A photographer captured this family scene of President Ulysses S. Grant, wife Julia, and son Jesse in 1872.

J̲ULIA AND U̲LYSSES S. G̲RANT, THE FIRST President to be elected following the Civil War, helped usher a new era and atmosphere into the recently reunited country. This period became known as the Gilded Age. It featured lavish spending (with an emphasis on quantity over quality) and widespread corruption (where behind-the-scenes influence helped one become rich). Both occurred during Grant's administration, with the spending drawing more admiration than criticism.

Julia had met her future husband and war hero when the West Point cadet visited her plantation home with her brother, Grant's fellow classmate. Her parents, Frederick and Ellen Wrenshall Dent, doubted the earning power of a soldier, and Grant's parents disapproved of the slave-holding Dents. The couple married anyway four years later. An almost nomadic life followed as Julia shadowed Grant's moves, even during parts of the Civil War.

Reaching the White House was a welcome change. Julia embraced her role as executive hostess, an approach that her successors generally mirrored. She entertained with enthusiasm. One elaborate dinner featured 29 courses of food. She turned the first White House wedding since the Tyler administration into a celebrity affair. Some 500 guests were invited to their daughter's wedding breakfast. Such events made great newspaper copy for the growing market of women readers. Society columns developed, and early female journalists shared gossip and fashion reports about life in the nation's capital with their eager readers.

Ulysses S. Grant wrote a bestselling autobiography near the end of his life that helped support his surviving family members. Julia went on to write her autobiography, too, although it was not published until seven decades after her death. This book is the earliest First Lady memoir to see print.

Because she had slightly crossed eyes, Julia Grant (left page) preferred to pose for photographs in profile rather than head on. Such a defect might have been "corrected" in portraits painted during an earlier era. Julia called her years in the White House her life's "happiest period." During that time the White House lawn was restricted to private use only. Previously it had been treated like a public park. Union soldiers had even camped there during the Civil War.

Lucy Hayes

THE HAYES ADMINISTRATION ★ 1877 – 1881

PRESIDENT	Rutherford B. Hayes (1822–1893), 19th President
MAIDEN NAME	Lucy Ware Webb
BORN	Aug. 28, 1831, in Chillicothe, Ohio
EDUCATION	Wesleyan Female College
WEDDING	Dec. 30, 1852
AGE AT MARRIAGE	21 years old
THEIR CHILDREN	Sardis (1853), James (1856), Rutherford (1858), Frances (1867), Scott (1871)
AGE AS FIRST LADY	45 years old
SPECIAL INTERESTS	Temperance
DIED	June 25, 1889, in Fremont, Ohio
AGE AT DEATH	57 years old
GRAVE	Spiegel Grove National Historic Landmark, Fremont, Ohio

Did You Know?

- The Hayeses' decision to refrain from serving alcohol at the White House reflected their personal religious preferences and a growing national movement of temperance, or restraint in the use of alcohol. Later on, Lucy would earn the nickname "Lemonade Lucy" for this White House custom.
- In an earlier era, soldiers in the Union Army gave the nickname "Mother Lucy" to this wife of their commanding officer.
- As a married woman, Lucy spoke less about the merits of women's rights than she had done when she was young and single. Opinions on the need for change were often hard to reconcile with the confines of married life in the 19th century.
- The White House was "purer because Mrs. Hayes had been its mistress," proclaimed a minister at the end of the Hayes administration.

LUCY HAYES WAS THE FIRST FIRST LADY to graduate from college. Her father, a physician named James Webb, died when she was two years old. Her mother, Maria Cook Webb, insisted that all three of her children, including her only daughter, receive a full education. At a time when many people debated the abilities of female students, Lucy was confident of their intelligence. "Woman's mind is as strong as man's — equal in all things and his superior in some," she observed.

Rutherford B. Hayes began calling on this bright, opinionated woman when her family moved to Cincinnati. The two were married after an 18-month-long engagement. Lucy bore eight children in the next 20 years; five of them lived to adulthood. When the Civil War, and later politics, took Hayes away from home, Lucy often went with him, even if it meant leaving her children with relatives.

When Hayes became President, two of their children were still young enough to move into the Executive Mansion with their parents. Perhaps the presence of these youngsters helped inspire their mother to establish the tradition of a public Easter egg roll on the White House lawn (an event held sporadically in earlier years).

Lucy's style as First Lady was considerably more subdued than her predecessors'. Most notable was the Hayeses' decision not to serve alcohol at White House events. Her interests in education reform and women's rights, and her involvement in the advancement of her husband's political career, brought a new dimension to the role of First Lady.

The Woman's Christian Temperance Union, a national organization that discouraged the drinking of alcohol, applauded the example Lucy and Rutherford B. Hayes (above) set by removing alcohol from the menu at White House social functions. In gratitude they commissioned a full-length portrait of Lucy (left page) that hangs today in the White House.

Lucretia Garfield

THE GARFIELD ADMINISTRATION ★ *1881*

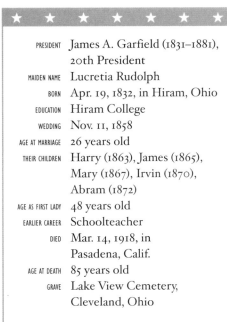

PRESIDENT	James A. Garfield (1831–1881), 20th President
MAIDEN NAME	Lucretia Rudolph
BORN	Apr. 19, 1832, in Hiram, Ohio
EDUCATION	Hiram College
WEDDING	Nov. 11, 1858
AGE AT MARRIAGE	26 years old
THEIR CHILDREN	Harry (1863), James (1865), Mary (1867), Irvin (1870), Abram (1872)
AGE AS FIRST LADY	48 years old
EARLIER CAREER	Schoolteacher
DIED	Mar. 14, 1918, in Pasadena, Calif.
AGE AT DEATH	85 years old
GRAVE	Lake View Cemetery, Cleveland, Ohio

Did You Know?

- Lucretia Garfield taught school during the early years of her marriage at a time when it was still unusual for married women to work.
- Tools of modern medicine like X-rays (for finding the assassin's bullet) and antibiotics (for fighting infections) could have saved the life of James A. Garfield.

"The wife of the President is the bravest woman in the universe."

— Newspaper commentary following the shooting of James A. Garfield in 1881

THE PRESIDENCY OF JAMES A. GARFIELD lasted only 199 days. More than a third of that time was expended with the President's slow and agonizing death, the result of an assassination attempt. His illness became the focus of his wife Lucretia's time in the White House. Between that calamity and her own serious bout of malaria in earlier months, there was little time for her to establish herself as First Lady.

Lucretia grew up on a farm in northeastern Ohio. Her parents were named Zebulon and Arabella Green Mason Rudolph. Lucretia met her future husband through local schools and attended what later became known as Hiram College. Their relationship took years to gel, even after a lengthy courtship. During their first five years of marriage, the newlyweds were separated for all but five months due to Garfield's military service and early political career. Lucretia's natural independence did not help either. Over time "Crete" curbed her assertive opinions and conformed to the customs of the era, slowly discarding her views on women's rights and equality.

Garfield's assassin is known to have stalked the President for weeks before firing what became a fatal shot. He claimed to have opted against shooting him when Garfield was escorting his ill wife out of Washington, D.C. "She clung so tenderly to the President's arm, that I did not have the heart to fire on him." After the President's death, Lucretia attended her husband's funeral—the first widow of a sitting President to do so.

Lucretia Garfield (left page) endured plenty of tearful moments while her husband's health failed because of an assassin's bullet. An artist suggested this bedside visit (above) by Lucretia and their only daughter Mary, then 14 years old.

Ellen Arthur

THE ARTHUR ADMINISTRATION ★ 1881 – 1885

PRESIDENT	Chester A. Arthur (1829–1886), 21st President
MAIDEN NAME	Ellen Lewis Herndon
BORN	Aug. 30, 1837, in Culpeper Court House, Va.
WEDDING	Oct. 25, 1859
AGE AT MARRIAGE	22 years old
THEIR CHILDREN	Chester (1864), Ellen (1871)
AGE AS FIRST LADY	Deceased
DIED	Jan. 12, 1880, in Albany, N.Y.
AGE AT DEATH	42 years old
GRAVE	Albany Rural Cemetery, Menands, N.Y.
ACTING FIRST LADY	Mary Arthur McElroy (President's sister)

Did You Know?

• Ellen Arthur's father earned fame with his death when, as captain of a passenger ship that caught in a storm off the coast of Florida, he successfully evacuated all aboard then sank with his doomed boat. That same year Ellen turned 20 years old.

As a widower, President Arthur turned to others to act as First Lady. His sister, Mary Arthur McElroy (above), stepped in periodically to serve as White House hostess.

CHESTER A. ARTHUR WAS STILL MOURNING the sudden loss of his wife, Ellen, when the death of James A. Garfield thrust him into the Presidency. Ellen had been raised with the Southern traditions of a prominent, pre-Civil War family from Virginia. Slaves were part of their property. Her father, William Lewis Herndon, was a noted U.S. naval officer who had once led an expedition up the Amazon River. Her mother, Frances Elizabeth Hansbrough Herndon, was a well-connected society figure. During a visit to New York City, Ellen was introduced to her future husband by a cousin (and roommate to Arthur). They were married several years later. The onset of the Civil War placed an early strain on their marriage, with Ellen favoring the cause of the South, unlike her Northern-born husband. Such tensions eased later on.

Pneumonia felled Ellen unexpectedly when she was just 42 years of age. After attending a concert in New York City, Ellen got chilled while waiting for her carriage to take her home, and she developed a cold. Her illness progressed quickly, and Arthur, who was out of town at the time, raced home only to find her unconscious. She never revived and was dead within two days of becoming ill. Ellen left behind two children. Their young daughter moved into the White House with her father when he became President, and the teenage son went off to school.

Arthur recruited his youngest sister to assist in the upbringing of young "Nell" and to act as occasional hostess. The mother of four children herself, Mary Arthur McElroy left her own family a few months each year in order to perform these favors. During his Presidency, Arthur reintroduced alcohol to social occasions in the White House. He never remarried. Arthur died at age 57 from kidney disease not even seven years after Ellen's death.

Ellen Arthur (left page) died 20 months before her husband became President. Later on Chester Arthur funded the installation of a stained glass window in Ellen's memory. The window was positioned in St. John's Episcopal Church (where his wife had sung in the choir), so that Arthur could see it from the White House at night.

Frances Cleveland

THE CLEVELAND ADMINISTRATIONS ★ *1885 – 1889* ★ *1893 – 1897*

PRESIDENT	Grover Cleveland (1837–1908), 22nd and 24th President
MAIDEN NAME	Frances Folsom
BORN	July 21, 1864, in Folsomville, N.Y.
EDUCATION	Wells College
WEDDING	June 2, 1886
AGE AT MARRIAGE	21 years old
THEIR CHILDREN	Ruth (1891), Esther (1893), Marion (1895), Richard (1897), Francis (1903)
AGE AS FIRST LADY	21 years old
LATER MARRIAGE	Thomas Jex Preston, Jr. (1880–1955), Feb. 10, 1913
DIED	Oct. 29, 1947, in Baltimore, Md.
AGE AT DEATH	83 years old
GRAVE	Princeton Cemetery, Princeton, N.J.
ACTING FIRST LADY	Rose Elizabeth Cleveland (President's sister)

Did You Know?

• The Clevelands are the only presidential couple to have their years of service interrupted by another President's administration.

Rose Elizabeth Cleveland (above) served as her brother's hostess until his marriage to Frances Folsom.

FRANCES CLEVELAND PACKED MANY FIRST LADY records into her life. At 21, she became the youngest one ever by marrying Grover Cleveland during his second year of office. She was the first (and only) First Lady to marry at the White House. During her husband's second term, she gave birth to the first (and only) presidential child born at the White House. Finally, she became the first widowed First Lady to remarry.

Her first marriage might have seemed unlikely to most who knew of Grover Cleveland and the fatherly role he had played toward Frances almost since her birth to his law partner Oscar Folsom and Emma Cornelia Harmon Folsom. Cleveland had actually bought the child's first baby carriage. His commitment to the youth deepened after the death of Frances's father when she was 11. Others who

knew of Cleveland's closeness to the family speculated that the nation's second bachelor President might marry Frances's mother, not the daughter who was 27 years his junior.

But marry they did, in full White House style, 15 months into Cleveland's first term of office. Despite her youth, Frances stepped into her role of First Lady with an assured confidence.

The former President died in 1908 when Frances was only 43. About five years later she remarried, choosing an archaeology professor from Princeton University. Her grave lies beside Cleveland's in New Jersey.

As First Lady, Frances Cleveland (left page) held weekly receptions on Saturday afternoons so working women could visit the White House. Frances gave birth to three children between or during her husband's two administrations. The family photo (above) was taken after the 1904 death of the Clevelands' first child at age 12 from diphtheria. The "Baby Ruth" candy bar is said to have been named in that girl's honor.

Caroline Harrison

THE BENJAMIN HARRISON ADMINISTRATION ★ *1889 – 1893*

PRESIDENT	Benjamin Harrison (1833–1901), 23rd President
MAIDEN NAME	Caroline Lavinia Scott
BORN	Oct. 1, 1832, in Oxford, Ohio
EDUCATION	Oxford Female Seminary
WEDDING	Oct. 20, 1853
AGE AT MARRIAGE	21 years old
THEIR CHILDREN	Russell (1854), Mary (1858)
AGE AS FIRST LADY	56 years old
DIED	Oct. 25, 1892, in Washington, D.C.
AGE AT DEATH	60 years old
GRAVE	Indianapolis, Ind.
ACTING FIRST LADY	Mary Scott Harrison McKee (daughter)
PRESIDENT'S OTHER WIVES	Mary Scott Lord Dimmick (1856–1948), second wife (married Apr. 6, 1896)
OTHER CHILDREN	Elizabeth (1897)

Did You Know?

- Caroline Harrison was one of three presidential wives to die during their husbands' administrations. The others were Letitia Tyler (in 1842) and Ellen Wilson (in 1914). All three Presidents remarried, two while still in office. Benjamin Harrison married later, choosing a widowed niece of his first wife.

"Imagine my whispering in your ear... all that could be delicate and affectionate."

— Benjamin Harrison,
letter to Caroline during his Civil War service

CAROLINE HARRISON WAS THE DAUGHTER of John Witherspoon Scott and Mary Potts Neal Scott. Her father was a Presbyterian minister and college educator. He introduced his daughter to her future husband, having met him through school. Benjamin Harrison, grandson of President William Henry Harrison, married Caroline some five years later. They were the last presidential couple to have their marriage interrupted by Civil War service.

As First Lady, Caroline took on the task of overhauling the White House. She arranged for upgrades to the plumbing, ordered old floors replaced, had the first electric lights installed (which she was afraid to switch on and off), and waged war against the mansion's rodent and insect inhabitants. Her interest in art led her to design a custom set of dishes for use during the Harrison Presidency. She established the White House china collection with examples of patterns used in previous administrations, too.

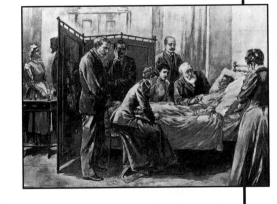

Near the end of her husband's administration, Caroline became ill with tuberculosis, then a common and incurable disease. She died two weeks before the presidential election that left her husband defeated. The Harrisons' daughter, Mary Scott Harrison McKee, stepped in as acting First Lady for the remaining months of the administration.

A few years later Harrison became the second former President to remarry. Millard Fillmore was the first.

During her White House years Caroline Harrison helped found the National Society of the Daughters of the American Revolution. She was its first president, too. After her death during Harrison's administration (shown above on her deathbed), the organization arranged for this portrait of Caroline (left page) to be painted and donated to the White House.

Ida McKinley

THE McKINLEY ADMINISTRATION ★ *1897 – 1901*

PRESIDENT	William McKinley (1843–1901), 25th President
MAIDEN NAME	Ida Saxton
BORN	June 8, 1847, in Canton, Ohio
EDUCATION	Brook Hall Seminary
WEDDING	Jan. 25, 1871
AGE AT MARRIAGE	23 years old
THEIR CHILDREN	Katherine (1872), Ida (1873); both died young
AGE AS FIRST LADY	49 years old
DIED	May 26, 1907, in Canton, Ohio
AGE AT DEATH	59 years old
GRAVE	McKinley National Memorial, Canton, Ohio

Did You Know?

• Ida McKinley handled the news of her husband's assassination and death in 1901 with surprising strength. "He is gone," she later said, "and life to me is dark now." Her own death came some six years after the President's. The McKinleys are buried in Canton, Ohio.

Emily Drayton Taylor painted this miniature likeness of Ida McKinley during her years in the White House.

IDA MCKINLEY'S LIFE BEGAN WITH GREAT PROMISE. She was the eldest daughter of banker James Asbury Saxton and Catherine Dewalt Saxton. Her childhood included a privileged education and a tour of Europe. She was so full of energy that her father made her a teller in his bank, an unusual responsibility for a woman at that time. She met her future husband at a church picnic, and William McKinley made frequent visits to her teller's window (often with flowers in hand as well as bank business) as their friendship developed. Upon their marriage, Ida's father presented the couple with a house.

The rosy picture did not last much longer. Two years into her marriage Ida lost in rapid succession a favorite grandfather, her mother, and an infant daughter. Her other child "Katie" caught typhoid fever and died in 1876. Depression ruled the days of the formerly rosy Ida. Her physical health declined, and she began to have epileptic seizures. Ida's mental and physical health never returned. She became an invalid, often sitting for hours occupied only by the task of crocheting endless pairs of slippers (literally thousands of them) that were given away to friends and for charity auctions.

William McKinley nursed and pampered his wife while managing to advance his political career, too. Ida struggled to meet the demands of being First Lady after her husband became President. McKinley adjusted White House custom so that, instead of sitting at the opposite end of the table, he could sit next to his wife and cover her face with his handkerchief if she began to have a small seizure. At times Ida was snappish and rude in public, but McKinley always doted on his First Lady.

After being shot by an assassin early in his second term, McKinley's earliest thoughts were about his wife. "My wife—be careful...how you tell her—oh, be careful!"

President McKinley and others were tight-lipped about the health of First Lady Ida McKinley (left page). They described her as prone to fainting spells and headaches. No mention was made of her actual condition, epilepsy, whose seizures were not well understood or controllable then.

FIRST LADIES
IN NAME
AND DEED

★ *1901 – 1933* ★

1904

Ida Tarbell's History of the Standard Oil Company *led to the trust-busting of John D. Rockefeller's oil empire.*

1911

The death of 146 seamstresses from the Triangle Shirtwaist Fire resulted in long-sought improvement to building codes and worker safety.

1916

Jeannette Rankin of Montana became the first woman elected to serve in the U.S. Congress as a member of the House of Representatives.

1917

Women began picketing the White House to demand the right to vote. Their nonviolent protests continued throughout the year despite threats, violence, jailings, and force-feedings in prison.

By the start of the 20th century the Presidents' wives assumed the role and title associated with the modern First Lady. Each woman served as her husband's hostess. Some took an interest in current affairs. Many committed time and energy to community service causes. Most brought career experiences of their own to their partnerships, as well as considerable political savvy. All experienced life in the public spotlight for themselves and coped with its impact on their families. Children and young adults were frequent participants in life at the White House during this era.

1920

The 19th Amendment was ratified, ending a 72-year-long fight for women to earn the right to vote nationwide.

1921

Margaret Sanger founded the American Birth Control League in an effort to promote family planning throughout the U.S.

1930

The Secret of the Old Clock debuted as the first installment in the Nancy Drew mystery series.

1932

Amelia Earhart became the first woman to fly alone across the Atlantic. Her flight from Newfoundland to Ireland came five years after Charles Lindbergh completed the same feat.

Edith Roosevelt

PRESIDENT	Theodore Roosevelt (1858–1919), 26th President
MAIDEN NAME	Edith Kermit Carow
BORN	Aug. 6, 1861, in Norwich, Conn.
WEDDING	Dec. 2, 1886
AGE AT MARRIAGE	25 years old
THEIR CHILDREN	Theodore (1887), Kermit (1889), Ethel (1891), Archibald (1894), Quentin (1897)
AGE AS FIRST LADY	40 years old
SPECIAL INTERESTS	Clothing for the poor
DIED	Sept. 30, 1948, in Oyster Bay, N.Y.
AGE AT DEATH	87 years old
GRAVE	Young's Memorial Cemetery, Oyster Bay, N.Y.
PRESIDENT'S OTHER WIVES	Alice Hathaway Lee (1861–1884), first wife (married Oct. 27, 1880)
OTHER CHILDREN	Alice (1884)

Did You Know?

• After the death of his first wife, Theodore Roosevelt tried to avoid meeting his childhood friend Edith Carow. She did the same. When they accidentally met in 1885, their mutual affections were rekindled, and the pair became secretly engaged. Their wedding followed about a year later.

• Edith Roosevelt's stepdaughter Alice was married at the White House in 1906.

"[Edith is] not only cultured but scholarly."

— President Theodore Roosevelt

THEODORE AND EDITH ROOSEVELT HAD BEEN married 14 years before he became President following the assassination of William McKinley. But Edith was not the 26th President's first wife. Alice, his first wife, died within four years of their marriage. She left behind an infant girl of the same name whom her stepmother later helped raise.

Although not his first wife, Edith was one of Roosevelt's oldest acquaintances. The daughter of merchant Charles Carow and Gertrude Elizabeth Tyler Carow, Edith had grown up in New York City as Roosevelt's next-door neighbor. She had been best friends with one of his sisters, and Roosevelt had at one time even proposed to her. Edith declined then but accepted when he approached her again years later.

Over the next ten years, the Roosevelt family swelled to include another daughter and four sons. All of these children, as well as a zoo-like assortment of pets, settled into the White House when the youthful President took office with his young First Lady. Their stay in the Executive Mansion is filled with tales of family roughhousing, practical jokes, and general silliness. Edith often referred to her playful husband as her sixth child.

Although longevity graced Edith's life (she lived to be 87), it did not favor her husband (who died at 60) or their sons. Three of their sons died during the two World Wars; only Archibald, although wounded in both, survived them. Among First Ladies, only Eliza Johnson and Edith Roosevelt lost children in combat.

Edith Roosevelt posed for this photo (above) with daughter Ethel during her husband's Presidency. Edith began the White House tradition of hanging portraits of the First Ladies along the ground-floor entryway to the Executive Mansion. Her portrait (left page) was painted in 1902.

Helen Taft

THE TAFT ADMINISTRATION ★ *1909 – 1913*

PRESIDENT	William Howard Taft (1857–1930), 27th President
MAIDEN NAME	Helen Herron
BORN	Jan. 2, 1861, in Cincinnati, Ohio
EDUCATION	Miami University (Ohio)
WEDDING	June 19, 1886
AGE AT MARRIAGE	25 years old
THEIR CHILDREN	Robert (1889), Helen (1891), Charles (1897)
AGE AS FIRST LADY	48 years old
DIED	May 22, 1943, in Washington, D.C.
AGE AT DEATH	82 years old
GRAVE	Arlington National Cemetery, Arlington, Va.

Did You Know?

• Helen Taft's nickname was Nellie.

• In 1911 the Tafts entertained 8,000 guests at their 25th wedding anniversary party. One visitor called it "the most brilliant function ever held" at the White House.

Keeping up with the latest inventions of the day, Helen Taft (above) tried her hand at cranking the film in an early movie camera.

HELEN TAFT'S FATHER, JOHN WILLIAMSON HERRON, had been a law partner of Rutherford B. Hayes. When President Hayes and his wife celebrated their 25th wedding anniversary at the White House in 1877, the guests included 16-year-old Helen, her father, and Helen's mother Harriet Collins Herron. This visit prompted Helen's interest in someday becoming First Lady. She met William Howard Taft at a bobsledding party in Cincinnati two years later. It took seven years and at least three proposals before Helen agreed to marry. Helen encouraged her lawyer husband to pursue politics instead of a courtroom career. This strategy eventually led the pair to the White House.

Helen's first act as First Lady established a shocking new precedent for executive spouses. Tradition had held that the outgoing President should escort the incoming one to the White House after Inauguration ceremonies. Knowing that Theodore Roosevelt planned to skip this formality, Helen maneuvered to seat herself in the place of honor beside her husband for his parade to the executive mansion.

A stroke put Helen at a disadvantage early in her husband's Presidency, robbing her of the power of speech for a time. She regained her health sufficiently to fulfill the traditional duties of First Lady and also to play an active role as an informal advisor and political partner to her husband. The Tafts, borrowing from the Hayes example, celebrated their own 25th wedding anniversary with an elaborate White House party.

The former presidential couple returned to Washington, D.C., eight years after Taft's administration ended when he was appointed Chief Justice of the Supreme Court, a job the old lawyer had wished to hold for years. Taft and his wife were the first presidential couple to be buried in Arlington National Cemetery. Only the Kennedys have joined them.

In 1910 Helen Taft posed wearing her inaugural gown for this portrait (left page). Helen left behind a lasting reminder of her years as First Lady by arranging to have 3,000 Japanese cherry trees planted around the Tidal Basin near the Jefferson Memorial.

Ellen Wilson

THE WILSON ADMINISTRATION ★ *1913 – 1921*

PRESIDENT	Woodrow Wilson (1856–1924), 28th President
MAIDEN NAME	Ellen Louise Axson
BORN	May 15, 1860, in Savannah, Ga.
EDUCATION	Female Seminary, Rome, Ga.
WEDDING	June 24, 1885
AGE AT MARRIAGE	25 years old
THEIR CHILDREN	Margaret (1886), Jessie (1887), Eleanor (1889)
AGE AS FIRST LADY	52 years old
SPECIAL INTERESTS	Improved housing in Washington, D.C.
EARLIER CAREER	Artist (painter)
DIED	Aug. 6, 1914, in Washington, D.C.
AGE AT DEATH	54 years old
GRAVE	Rome, Ga.
ACTING FIRST LADY	Margaret Woodrow Wilson (daughter), Helen Bones (President's cousin)
PRESIDENT'S OTHER WIVES	*see next page*

Did You Know?

• Ellen Wilson and Letitia Tyler are the only First Ladies not buried with their husbands.

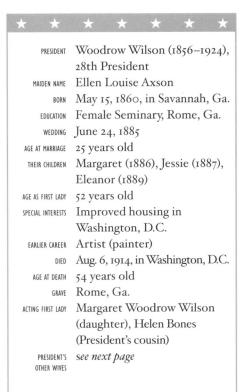

Ellen planned White House weddings for two of her three daughters (above). The third helped with hostess duties after Ellen became ill.

LIKE JOHN TYLER, WOODROW WILSON not only lost one wife during his Presidency but gained a new one, as well. He and his first wife Ellen had been married 27 years when they moved into the White House. Although the couple met as children, they did not begin courting until Ellen was 22 years old. By then Ellen's mother, Margaret Hoyt Axson, was dead, and Ellen was helping her father, Samuel Edward Axson, raise her younger siblings. Both her father and Wilson's were Presbyterian ministers.

Another two years passed before Ellen and Wilson were married. At that point he had become a professor at Bryn Mawr College, and she had studied art in New York City with an eye toward painting professionally. Although Ellen continued to paint throughout her life, the births of three daughters and her support of Wilson's academic and then political careers took precedence over her own.

As First Lady, Ellen set a precedent followed by many subsequent wives of Presidents. She not only identified a particular cause of special interest (as had Lucy Hayes, for example) but she lobbied Congress to support her work, too. Ellen became the guiding hand in raising awareness about slum housing in the nation's capital.

Ellen became ill with Bright's Disease, a kidney ailment, in 1914. Congress rushed to pass what was known as "Mrs. Wilson's Bill" to improve housing among the area's poor. By the fall she was dead. The President was devastated, privately admitting he would welcome assassination. No such fate befell him. Instead, some seven months after his wife's death, he met the next Mrs. Wilson.

Ellen Wilson (left page) and her daughters set the precedent of family members attending presidential addresses of Congress. Ellen, an accomplished artist (above), established a painting studio for herself in the White House and sold some of her artwork. Profits went to charities.

Edith Wilson

THE WILSON ADMINISTRATION ★ 1913 – 1921

PRESIDENT	Woodrow Wilson (1856–1924), 28th President
MAIDEN NAME	Edith Bolling
BORN	Oct. 15, 1872, in Wytheville, Va.
EDUCATION	Martha Washington College
WEDDING	Dec. 18, 1915
AGE AT MARRIAGE	43 years old
THEIR CHILDREN	None
AGE AS FIRST LADY	43 years old
CAREER	Managed family jewelry business
PREVIOUS MARRIAGE	Norman Galt (1862–1908), Apr. 30, 1896
DIED	Dec. 28, 1961, in Washington, D.C.
AGE AT DEATH	89 years old
GRAVE	Washington National Cathedral, Washington, D.C.
ACTING FIRST LADY	Helen Bones (President's cousin)
PRESIDENT'S OTHER WIVES	*see previous page*

Did You Know?

- Edith counted Pocahontas among her distant relatives, making her the only First Lady to claim Native American ancestry.

A future as First Lady would have seemed like an improbable dream—if it was imagined at all—for Edith Bolling at age 15 (above).

THE VERY WOMAN WOODROW WILSON asked to assist him after the death of his first wife in 1914 became the person to introduce him to his future second wife the following year. Wilson's cousin, Helen Bones, was already familiar with the workings of the White House, having served as social secretary to the first Mrs. Wilson. One of her friends, a widow named Edith Bolling Galt, happened to be visiting Helen at the White House when bad weather brought the President home early from a golf game. The three sat down for tea in a chance encounter that quickly blossomed into romance. Edith and Wilson were married before the year was out.

The second Mrs. Wilson had grown up in a privileged home, the daughter of a judge named William Holcombe Bolling and his wife, Sallie White Bolling. Edith had been married 12 years to a prosperous jewelry store owner when he died suddenly. Their one child had died, too. Seven years later she met and married President Wilson.

As First Lady, Edith is most remembered for the role she played near the end of Wilson's administration. A stroke left the President gravely ill with 18 months left in his second term. Doctors instructed Edith to shelter him from as much strain as possible in order to aid his recovery. Edith did just that, setting herself up as an impenetrable wall between the President and other people and paperwork. By limiting him to only the most essential tasks, she helped Wilson complete his Presidency. In so doing, however, she opened herself up to criticism of overreaching her place as a President's wife, a charge still leveled today.

This portrait of Edith Wilson (left page) was painted soon after she became the President's second wife, and thus First Lady. Although her marriage to Woodrow Wilson (commemorated above) was cut short by his death after eight years, and even though she outlived him by nearly four decades, Edith Wilson chose to be buried by this husband, not her earlier one.

Florence Harding

THE HARDING ADMINISTRATION ★ *1921 – 1923*

PRESIDENT	Warren G. Harding (1865–1923), 29th President
MAIDEN NAME	Florence Mabel Kling
BORN	Aug. 15, 1860, in Marion, Ohio
WEDDING	July 8, 1891
AGE AT MARRIAGE	30 years old
THEIR CHILDREN	None
AGE AS FIRST LADY	60 years old
EARLIER CAREER	Journalism
PREVIOUS MARRIAGE AND CHILD	Henry DeWolfe (1859–1894), March 1880 (ended in divorce); Marshall (1880)
DIED	Nov. 21, 1924, in Marion, Ohio
AGE AT DEATH	64 years old
GRAVE	Harding Memorial, Marion, Ohio

Did You Know?

• Florence Harding was the first divorcée to serve as First Lady. Rachel Jackson, who was also divorced, died before reaching the White House. Betty Ford was the only other divorcée who became First Lady.

President and Mrs. Harding (above, left and center) strolled the grounds of the U.S. Naval Academy in Annapolis, Maryland, during a presidential visit.

WHEN FLORENCE HARDING ENTERED the White House in 1921, she was the oldest woman yet (at age 60) to take on the duties of First Lady. She was also older than her husband was (by more than five years), a presidential seniority gap that has never been topped.

Florence married both of her husbands despite the objections of her father, a prominent local banker. Her parents were Amos and Louisa Bouton Kling. Florence's first marriage ended when her husband deserted her and their young son. They later divorced, he died young, and Florence's parents took over custody of her child (who died himself as a young man).

When Florence first spied Warren G. Harding, he was a relative newcomer in her small town, having just bought an ownership stake in the local newspaper. Before the next year was out, they had married. (Her father did not speak to her for seven years.) Soon after the wedding, Florence took on management responsibilities at her new husband's paper. When Harding turned to government service a few years later, she helped manage his political career, too. She encouraged him to make the White House his ultimate career goal and then helped him reach it.

As First Lady she brought a new level of openness to the White House. Visitors were welcome to stroll again on its grounds and to drop by the Executive Mansion for tours. On New Year's Days Florence willingly stood in receiving lines for hours until every visitor for the traditional open house had been greeted. At the same time, the President and his wife were tight-lipped about personal matters, including their own fragile healths and the President's romantic affair (and illegitimate child) with another woman. Citizens were stunned not only by Harding's sudden death during the third year of his administration, but by the death of Florence just over a year later. Only First Lady Eliza Johnson died more quickly after a presidential husband's death.

Florence Harding (left page) used makeup, one of the first First Ladies to do so. Cosmetics helped her conceal her age difference with the President (he was five years younger) and present a more youthful image as First Lady.

Grace Coolidge

THE COOLIDGE ADMINISTRATION ★ *1923 – 1929*

PRESIDENT	Calvin Coolidge (1872–1933), 30th President
MAIDEN NAME	Grace Anna Goodhue
BORN	Jan. 3, 1879, in Burlington, Vt.
EDUCATION	University of Vermont
WEDDING	Oct. 4, 1905
AGE AT MARRIAGE	26 years old
THEIR CHILDREN	John (1906), Calvin (1908)
AGE AS FIRST LADY	44 years old
EARLIER CAREER	Schoolteacher for the deaf
DIED	July 8, 1957, in Northampton, Mass.
AGE AT DEATH	78 years old
GRAVE	Plymouth Notch Cemetery, Plymouth, Vt.

Did You Know?
• Grace Coolidge kept a pet raccoon at the White House.

Calvin and Grace Coolidge rode together (above) to his Inauguration in 1925. His second swearing in was more festive (coming after an election) than his first (following the unexpected death of Warren G. Harding).

IT IS ONLY FITTING THAT THE FIRST MEETING of Grace and Calvin Coolidge was a funny one. The couple who became known for their playful wit caught their first glimpse of one another when Grace looked up from watering a garden to see Coolidge through an open window of a nearby building. He was shaving, wearing only his long underwear and a dress hat. She burst out laughing at the sight, he looked over and saw her, and the introduction that followed cemented their relationship.

Although the pair met in Massachusetts, they were both natives of Vermont. Grace's parents were Andrew Issachar Goodhue, an engineer and steamboat inspector, and Lemira Barrett Goodhue. Grace was the first First Lady to graduate from a coeducational college or university. Then she took further courses to prepare for a career in the education of the deaf, an interest that she pursued for the rest of her life. Her first job was teaching the deaf how to read lips.

Following the sudden death of Warren G. Harding, the Coolidges brought a New England style of natural simplicity to their years in the White House. The celebration of Charles Lindbergh's first transatlantic flight proved to be a high point. The bizarre death of their youngest son was a low. (The 16-year-old played tennis without wearing socks, got a blister, developed blood poisoning, and died, all in a matter of a few days.)

After leaving the White House, Grace probably spoke for many First Ladies. "This was I and yet not I," she said of her role. "This was the wife of the President of the United States and she took precedence over me."

Calvin Coolidge loved to buy clothes for his wife (above, she stands on a White House balcony). He sulked if she wore an evening gown more than once. She posed for her official portrait (left page) in a simple yet elegant full-length view, joined by her collie Rob Roy.

Lou Hoover

THE HOOVER ADMINISTRATION ★ *1929 – 1933*

PRESIDENT	Herbert Hoover (1874–1964), 31st President
MAIDEN NAME	Lou Henry
BORN	Mar. 29, 1874, in Waterloo, Iowa
EDUCATION	Stanford University
WEDDING	Feb. 10, 1899
AGE AT MARRIAGE	24 years old
THEIR CHILDREN	Herbert (1903), Allan (1907)
AGE AS FIRST LADY	54 years old
EARLIER CAREER	Geologist
DIED	Jan. 7, 1944, in New York, N.Y.
AGE AT DEATH	69 years old
GRAVE	Herbert Hoover National Historic Site, West Branch, Iowa

Did You Know?

• Lou and Herbert Hoover used Chinese as their private language during their White House years.

• The Hoovers won a gold award from the Mining and Metallurgical Society for their translation of a 16th-century Latin geology text.

Lou Hoover (above) relaxes at home following her years as First Lady.

THE ADVENTURESOME LIFESTYLE of Lou Hoover's youth became good preparation for her adult life. Midway through her childhood, she moved with her parents, banker Charles Delano Henry and Florence Ida Weed Henry, from Iowa to southern California. Her childhood featured camping expeditions, horseback riding, hunting trips, practice with taxidermy, and rock hunting. It's little wonder that one of her favorite organizations later on was the Girl Scouts, a group she headed for a time.

In 1894 she entered Stanford University as a geology student, the first woman ever to do so, and it was there that she met Herbert Hoover, a senior in the program. They married after her graduation and embarked on more than a decade of global travel through her husband's career as a mining geologist. Lou gave birth to two sons during this period, learning Chinese and several other foreign languages on the side. Although Lou never worked as a geologist, she did serve as equal partner with her husband in their five-year effort to translate an important historical text about metallurgy, the study of metals.

Lou brought many innovations to her years as First Lady. She developed a catalog of historic White House furnishings. She gave nationally broadcast radio addresses. She even ended the custom that kept pregnant women out of White House receiving lines. Perhaps Hoover's election loss in 1932 and the nation's deepening economic crisis led the Hoovers to skip the traditional New Year's Day open house in 1933. They traveled instead.

Herbert Hoover was already working in China when his future wife (standing, above, during her college years with friend Marian Dole and her sister, Jean Henry, at right) graduated from Stanford University. He sent her a wedding proposal by telegram. Lou cabled back with her acceptance. Lou Hoover's official portrait (left page) is a copy of one owned by the Hoovers.

LIVES OF PUBLIC SERVICE

★ *1933 – 1981* ★

1933

Hattie Caraway, newly elected Senator from Arkansas, joined the U.S. Senate as its first woman to earn outright election to the legislative body.

1939

Marian Anderson overcame racial discrimination by the Daughters of the American Revolution to present an open-air concert in Washington, D.C., at the Lincoln Memorial.

1941 – 1945

Women supported the efforts of World War II by entering the labor force at jobs traditionally held by men. Rosie the Riveter and thousands like her welded, cast, and manufactured the way to victory.

1953

Simone de Beauvoir's The Second Sex was published in the U.S., highlighting the continued inequality of women around the globe.

As the century progressed, the role of a political wife evolved into a lifetime commitment to public service. Future Presidents pursued a variety of elected offices on the road to the White House, with wives and families falling increasingly within the glare of public scrutiny. The role of First Lady expanded into a job-like experience, complete with professional staff support and calendars packed with travel, speeches, and fundraising. Even after leaving the office behind, former First Ladies remained influential with the public and involved in community causes.

1955

The refusal of Rosa Parks to yield her seat to a white person on a segregated bus sparked the year-long Montgomery bus boycott and the modern Civil Rights Movement.

1962

The publication of Rachel Carson's Silent Spring *prompted the development of expanded efforts at conservation and environmental protection.*

1972

The passage of Title IX legislation by the U.S. Congress revolutionized the access of girls and young women to equal opportunities in athletics and education.

1973

The Supreme Court's Roe v. Wade *decision removed restrictions on a woman's right to use abortion to terminate a pregnancy during its first trimester.*

Eleanor Roosevelt

THE FRANKLIN D. ROOSEVELT ADMINISTRATION ★ 1933 – 1945

Did You Know?

• Following the death of her husband, Eleanor Roosevelt learned that he had begun seeing his former mistress again and was with her when he died. Other 20th century First Ladies faced with philandering husbands include Florence Harding, Mamie Eisenhower, Jackie Kennedy, Lady Bird Johnson, and Hillary Clinton.

> "...no matter how plain a woman may be if truth and loyalty are stamped upon her face all will be attracted to her."
>
> — Eleanor Roosevelt, *age 14*

ELEANOR ROOSEVELT EXPANDED THE ROLE of First Lady into a rainbow of new dimensions. In the process she established yardsticks by which those who followed her to the White House would almost inevitably be measured. She is the nation's longest-serving First Lady because her husband was the longest-serving President. (He won four elections and held office just over 12 years in all.) Eleanor pioneered a new level of activism for former First Ladies, too.

The role that Eleanor assumed during adulthood was light-years away from her tentative, reserved childhood. Her parents were named Elliott Roosevelt and Anna Livingston Hall Roosevelt. Eleanor was always shy, forever feeling awkward. Her mother died when she was eight. Her father, whom she adored, was often absent because of problems with alcoholism. By the time she was ten, he had died, too. Not until Eleanor was sent to an English boarding school in her mid-teens did she find an environment and role models that helped her begin to overcome her lack of self-confidence.

Eleanor had only recently returned to the United States when she bumped into a distant and rarely seen cousin during a train ride: Franklin D. Roosevelt. The chance encounter led to love and, within three years, marriage. Eleanor was given away at her wedding by her father's older brother, a man who just happened at that time to be President of the United States—Theodore Roosevelt. (Eleanor was his favorite niece.)

This multifaceted portrait (left page) was painted of Eleanor Roosevelt about five years after she left the White House. She was 65 years old and almost as active in her retirement years as she had been as First Lady. The artist, Douglas Chandor, sought to capture Eleanor's energy and range of talents in the portrait. Eleanor's face has even graced postage stamps (above, a 1984 issue).

"The future
is literally
in our hands
to mold as we like.
But we cannot wait
until tomorrow.
Tomorrow is now."

— Eleanor Roosevelt, *Tomorrow Is Now*,
published after her death

The early years of Eleanor's marriage to Franklin followed the usual conventions of the day. There were many pregnancies (six in 11 years), with five children surviving infancy. Eleanor quit her pre-marriage volunteer work. When it came to matters of household management, she deferred to her overbearing mother-in-law, who lived next door.

Then several experiences contributed to Eleanor's growing independence. One was World War I, an event that brought increased opportunities and responsibilities to many women. Another was the shock of learning that her husband was involved romantically with another woman. The affair ended, and their marriage survived, but Eleanor began to think more about meeting her own needs, not just those of the people around her. An additional factor was her husband contracting polio in 1921, a disease that left him crippled

for the rest of his life. Eleanor encouraged his recovery—and at the same time built her own confidence—by doing the political legwork that helped him gain elected office.

This political partnership would last for the rest of their marriage, and it eventually landed them in the White House. Their lengthy stay there coincided with some of the most challenging years of the 20th century, including the Great Depression and World War II. Such events placed greater demands than ever on the Presidency. The combination of Eleanor's growing independence, her increased leadership as partner to a disabled husband, and the demands of the times set the stage for Eleanor to become the most active First Lady yet seen.

Precedents fell by the wayside, and new ones took their places. Gone was the limiting view of First Lady as little more than hostess. Eleanor, who had already served as "eyes and

ears" for her wheelchair-bound husband, extended her habit of traveling in his place. She spoke on his behalf at the Democratic Party Convention, stood in for him at meetings with interest groups, and traveled abroad as his representative. She supported her own causes more publicly and persistently than had any other First Lady—from labor rights for women to greater rights for children to civil rights for African Americans. She lobbied privately with her husband on other points—such as bringing more women into the government. (Roosevelt agreed, appointing the first woman to a presidential Cabinet, among many other gains.)

Eleanor established the First Lady tradition of meeting with reporters by holding weekly press conferences, some 348 sessions in all by the time her tenure had ended. Following a suggestion from journalist and close friend Lorena Hickok, Eleanor made the events women-only thus creating jobs for female reporters. Eleanor kept in touch with the reading public directly, too, through a weekly column, "My Day," that was printed in newspapers across the country.

"The story is over," Eleanor stated following the sudden death of her husband just three months into his fourth term of office. In fact, the story of her own involvement in public service was not over. Two Presidents—Harry S. Truman and John F. Kennedy—appointed her to represent the United States as part of its delegation to the United Nations. In that capacity she helped draft the Universal Declaration of Human Rights. The same values of mutual respect that guided her own life helped frame this vision for the wider world.

Eleanor and Franklin Roosevelt (left page, bottom, with their four sons) were the first presidential couple to host a visit to the United States by British monarchs. Eleanor and Queen Elizabeth, wife of King George VI (left page, top), made an open-car appearance during the 1939 event. Eleanor remained active in politics even after Franklin's death. In 1960 she made a supportive appearance (above) for presidential candidate John F. Kennedy (at left) and his running mate Lyndon B. Johnson. The Democratic pair won the election soon after.

Bess Truman

THE TRUMAN ADMINISTRATION ★ 1945 – 1953

PRESIDENT	Harry S. Truman (1884–1972), 33rd President
MAIDEN NAME	Elizabeth Virginia Wallace
BORN	Feb. 13, 1885, in Independence, Mo.
WEDDING	June 28, 1919, in Independence, Mo.
AGE AT MARRIAGE	34 years old
THEIR CHILDREN	Margaret (1924)
AGE AS FIRST LADY	60 years old
EARLIER CAREER	Secretary
DIED	Oct. 18, 1982, in Independence, Mo.
AGE AT DEATH	97 years old
GRAVE	Independence, Mo.

Did You Know?

- The Trumans postponed their marriage while Bess cared for her family and completed her education. Harry Truman's military service during World War I was an added delay.
- Presidential staffers referred to the close-knit Truman family trio of Harry, Bess, and their college-aged daughter as the "three musketeers."
- White House renovations forced the First Family to live elsewhere during Truman's second term.

> ## "I never make a report or deliver a speech without her editing it."

— Harry S. Truman, *commenting on the role Bess Truman played on his U.S. Senate staff*

BESS AND HARRY S. TRUMAN RACKED UP the longest courtship in presidential history, and that's without counting the fact that the couple first met during a Sunday School class when she was only five and he was just six. They began writing letters to one another during their late teens, but some 15 years and a World War passed before the pair were married. By then both of them were in their 30s.

When Bess was 18, her father, David Willock Wallace, a local government official, killed himself. Bess was left with her mother, Madge Gates Wallace, and her three younger siblings. Bess grew up as a talented athlete. She excelled at tennis, baseball, basketball, fencing, ice skating, even the shot put. Truman was so devoted in wooing Bess that he built her a place to play tennis.

The Trumans moved into the White House following the death of Franklin D. Roosevelt. As with every other First Lady, Bess established her own interpretation of the job, all the while trying not to be too intimidated by her predecessor's example. She canceled Eleanor Roosevelt's traditional press conferences (eventually Bess agreed to answer written questions for inquisitive reporters), took trains instead of planes (judging trains to be more dignified), and declined all public speaking opportunities (she preferred to be in the background).

By living to 97 years of age, Bess set one final presidential record. No other First Lady ever lived so long.

Elizabeth "Bess" Wallace (above) grew up with three younger brothers in Independence, Missouri, the same hometown as her future husband. The official portrait of Bess Truman (left page) was copied from a painting owned by the Trumans.

Mamie Eisenhower

THE EISENHOWER ADMINISTRATION ★ *1953 – 1961*

PRESIDENT	Dwight D. Eisenhower (1890–1969), 34th President
MAIDEN NAME	Mamie Geneva Doud
BORN	Nov. 14, 1896, in Boone, Iowa
WEDDING	July 1, 1916
AGE AT MARRIAGE	19 years old
THEIR CHILDREN	John (1922)
AGE AS FIRST LADY	56 years old
DIED	Nov. 1, 1979, in Washington, D.C.
AGE AT DEATH	82 years old
GRAVE	Eisenhower Center, Abilene, Kans.

Did You Know?

• During the Eisenhower administration the U.S. Congress finally replaced the ragtag series of prior pension plans for presidential widows with a comprehensive program. Until then pensions had been granted in varying amounts to hit-or-miss lists of widows. The new law stated that any widow (present and future) of a former President was entitled to a pension, and it set a value for the stipend of $10,000 per year. That amount was later increased to $20,000 in 1971, but it has not been changed since.

Over the years the images of Presidents and First Ladies have graced everything from political campaign buttons to unofficial product endorsements to paper dolls to salt and pepper shakers (above, Mamie and Dwight D. Eisenhower).

WHEN MAMIE AND DWIGHT D. EISENHOWER reached the White House after 36 years of marriage, they created their own personal record. The White House was the first home the couple ever moved into with any kind of permanency. Up until then, thanks to Eisenhower's previous military career, they had moved at least 27 times.

Mamie met her future husband when he was a 25-year-old second lieutenant in the U.S. Army. She was only 18 and was staying with her parents, John Sheldon Doud, a meat packer, and Elivera Carlson Doud, at the family's winter home in Texas. (The rest of the year they lived in Denver, Colorado.)

By the time Eisenhower became President, Mamie was a practiced hostess. At home in the White House, Mamie helped host a seemingly endless parade of foreign dignitaries for state visits. She shook hands with thousands of other visitors, often greeting hundreds of strangers a day. She added the first official staff member to the First Lady's office, the "acting secretary to the President's wife." The Eisenhowers relaxed at the Executive Mansion, too. "At last I've got a job where I can stay home nights, and, by golly, I'm going to stay home," observed the President.

The Eisenhowers retired to a farm in Pennsylvania following their eight-year stay at the White House. "Whenever Ike went away, the house sagged," Mamie observed about their years together in the only house they ever owned. "When he came home, the house was alive again."

Mamie Eisenhower (left page and above with her husband and victory headlines in 1952) chose an Inaugural gown in her favorite color, a shade that became widely known as "Mamie pink." Her bangs became a fashion trademark, too. A trend follower as well as a trendsetter, the First Lady was content to wear costume jewelry (imitation versions of real pearls and jewels) and eat family suppers on TV trays, just like average Americans of the day.

Jacqueline Kennedy

PRESIDENT	John F. Kennedy (1917–1963), 35th President
MAIDEN NAME	Jacqueline Lee Bouvier
BORN	July 28, 1929, in Southampton, N.Y.
EDUCATION	Vassar College, George Washington University
WEDDING	Sept. 12, 1953
AGE AT MARRIAGE	24 years old
THEIR CHILDREN	Caroline (1957), John (1960)
AGE AS FIRST LADY	31 years old
SPECIAL INTERESTS	Historic preservation, the arts
EARLIER CAREER	Professional photographer
LATER CAREERS	Book editor, advocate for historic preservation
LATER MARRIAGE	Aristotle Socrates Onassis (1906–1975), Oct. 20, 1968
DIED	May 19, 1994, in New York, N.Y.
AGE AT DEATH	64 years old
GRAVE	Arlington National Cemetery, Arlington, Va.

Did You Know?

• In 1953, even before their engagement, John F. Kennedy and his future First Lady attended an Eisenhower Inaugural ball.

"The one thing
I do not
want to be called
is First Lady.
It sounds like
a saddle horse."

— Jacqueline Kennedy
to her White House secretary

JUST AS JOHN F. KENNEDY INTRODUCED a youthful spirit to the Presidency, Jacqueline Kennedy likewise did the same for the role of the First Lady. She was just 31 years old when she became First Lady. Only Frances Cleveland and Julia Tyler came to the post at a younger age than did the woman who became affectionately known to the nation as "Jackie." Her husband (whom many called "Jack") was, at age 43, the youngest man ever elected President. (Theodore Roosevelt became President at a younger age, but through succession, not election.)

Jackie was the first First Lady to be born in the 20th century. Her parents were the stockbroker John Vernou Bouvier III and Janet Norton Lee Bouvier. They divorced the year that Jackie turned 11. Her mother remarried two years later. Jackie's stepfather, Hugh Auchincloss, was quite wealthy, and Jackie enjoyed a privileged childhood with private schools, horseback riding, and multiple family homes. She attended Vassar College, studied abroad in Paris, and earned a bachelor's degree in art from George Washington University. Jackie had become a professional pho-

tographer in Washington, D.C., by the time she met her future husband, then a U.S. Senator, at a dinner party in 1951. Their wedding was a society affair with 800 guests, extensive media coverage, and a blessing sent by the Pope.

One pregnancy failed before the birth of the first Kennedy child, daughter Caroline. John, Jr., followed in late 1960, arriving after his father had won the presidential election, but

Jacqueline Kennedy posed for this portrait (left page) in 1970, a decade after her husband was elected President. The youthful First Lady (pictured above, after her death, on the cover of Time *magazine) had set new precedents for independence by traveling for fun without the President. Her adventures led her to such places as the Mediterranean, India, and Italy.*

before his Inauguration. Caroline and John became the first small children of a President to move into the White House since Theodore Roosevelt's administration.

The new First Lady juggled the demands of motherhood with social duties and her commitment to several key interests. Her efforts were aided by a growing staff in the office of the First Lady. At times she recruited Lady Bird Johnson, the Vice President's wife, to fill in for her at social functions. She insisted that her children's lives remain a private matter, not an easy task to accomplish given the public's eagerness for any and all news about this youthful First Family. Even if news about the children was scarce, "Jack and Jackie" were themselves idolized and imitated. The "Jackie look" set fashion trends in everything from hairstyles to dress lengths to the wearing of hats.

Even before her husband's Inauguration, Jackie declared her intention to restore the historic style of the White House. Her pre-Inaugural announcement became a precedent for other First Ladies-to-be. Once in the White House, Jackie used her interest in art history to direct the research, fundraising, and effort necessary for a full-scale redecoration of the Executive Mansion. The classic White House look that today's visitors take as a given was established under her leadership. Antiques, period wallpaper, and extensive use of art all brought a unified elegance to the home. The mansion's first guidebooks were developed at this time, both to explain the significance of the collection and to help fund its preservation. When the project was completed in early 1962, Jackie led the nation on a televised one-hour tour of the White House. No First Lady had ever made such extensive use of this newest medium of communication. Jackie promoted the performing arts with equal enthusiasm during her tenure.

Although Jackie often stayed behind during her husband's frequent travels, circumstance placed them together on Kennedy's ill-fated trip to Texas in November 1963. The two were seated side-by-side in a convertible—one of several vehicles in a presidential motorcade through the streets of Dallas—when shots rang out. The President was mortally wounded and never regained consciousness. In less than an hour he was dead. Soon after, Lyndon B. Johnson was sworn in as President in a makeshift ceremony aboard the presidential plane. Jackie Kennedy stood beside Johnson, wearing the same outfit she had worn earlier in the day. Now it was stained with her dead husband's blood. She is the only presidential widow to attend the swearing in of her husband's successor.

In the days and years that followed, Jackie did much to ensure that her husband would be well remembered. She dictated details for his funeral that made it solemn and memorable—

"...if you bungle raising your children, I don't think whatever else you do well matters very much."

— Jacqueline Kennedy

from the use of the horse-drawn caisson that carried the body to the presence of a riderless horse in the procession. Her own bearing and that of her young children during the public events won sympathy and admiration from around the world. As time passed, she devoted much energy to the development of Kennedy's presidential library.

But Jackie did not remain a widow. Only 34 years old when her husband died, she was remarried before she turned 40. Her second husband was a wealthy shipowner from Greece named Aristotle Onassis. He was 23 years older than Jackie. Their marriage lasted until his death in 1975. Then Jackie moved to New York City and developed a career in book publishing. No other former First Lady had worked full-time before then. She collaborated on historic preservation projects, too.

When she died of cancer some two decades later, her son recalled her commitment to a "love of words, the bonds of home and family, and her spirit of adventure."

Jackie chose to be buried beside her first husband at Arlington National Cemetery. The Kennedys' graves are joined by those of their infant son and a stillborn daughter. An everlasting flame marks the site, overlooking the nation's capital. The President's assassinated brother, Robert F. Kennedy, rests nearby. The Kennedys' son, John F. Kennedy, Jr., was killed in an airplane crash in 1999. His ashes were scattered at sea.

Perhaps not since the time of Mary Todd Lincoln had joys and sorrows so punctuated the life of a First Lady as they did for Jacqueline Kennedy. Happier days such as her wedding (left page) and husband's election contrasted with the loss at infancy of a son while she was First Lady. Then, just three months later, her husband was felled by an assassin's bullet. During the Kennedy Presidency a curious public enjoyed scenes from their domestic (above, left) and official lives (above, center). After grieving the loss of her husband in 1963, Jackie found herself back in the spotlight (above, right) following the assassination not even five years later of her husband's brother Robert.

Lady Bird Johnson

THE LYNDON B. JOHNSON ADMINISTRATION ★ 1963 – 1969

PRESIDENT	Lyndon B. Johnson (1908–1973), 36th President
MAIDEN NAME	Claudia Alta Taylor
BORN	Dec. 22, 1912, in Karnack, Tex.
EDUCATION	University of Texas
WEDDING	Nov. 17, 1934
AGE AT MARRIAGE	21 years old
THEIR CHILDREN	Lynda (1944), Luci (1947)
AGE AS FIRST LADY	50 years old
SPECIAL INTEREST	Beautification of cities and highways
CAREERS	Radio broadcasting, family businesses

Did You Know?

• Lady Bird Johnson has outlived her presidential husband longer than any other First Lady except for Sarah Polk (42 years) and Frances Cleveland (40 years). In 2005 Lady Bird eclipsed Lucretia Garfield's record of 36 years.

"Beauty in nature nourishes us and brings joy to the human spirit," observed Lady Bird Johnson (above), founder of the National Wildflower Research Center.

CLAUDIA ALTA TAYLOR EARNED HER NICKNAME as a baby when she was pronounced as "pretty as a ladybird" by a caregiver. She became known as "Lady Bird" forever after. Her mother, Minnie Lee Pattillo Taylor, died when Lady Bird was just five years old, and the girl was raised by an aunt and her father, a rancher and merchant named Thomas Jefferson Taylor. Lady Bird excelled at school. By the time she met her future husband at age 21, she had already graduated near the top of her class from the University of Texas, earning a teaching certificate in addition to majoring in journalism.

Lyndon B. Johnson fell in love with Lady Bird at once. He was introduced to her by a mutual friend one night and proposed to her the next day. Johnson applied what would later become his legendary powers of persuasion, and the couple were wed before two months had passed. Over the years Lady Bird would help advance her husband's political career as his partner, his financial backer, and an unpaid office manager (taking charge of it entirely when war and illness twice took Johnson away from the U.S. Congress). She established her own professional life, too, as the owner of a growing radio broadcasting company.

Lady Bird expanded the definition of the First Lady's role through her tireless promotion of two causes: her husband and the natural beauty of America. In support of the first, she campaigned more extensively than had any other First Lady. As for the latter, she tirelessly promoted passage of the Highway Beautification Act that helped reduce the clutter of billboards and roadside junkyards along the nation's highways. Years later she encouraged the planting and preservation of wildflowers, a successful effort that she supports to this day from her home in Texas.

The professionalism of the office of First Lady was completed during Lady Bird Johnson's tenure (left page, her official portrait). More than a dozen staff members helped support what had become a full-time job. The former First Lady's leadership on beautification was recognized when the Redwood National Park established the Lady Bird Johnson Grove in her honor.

Pat Nixon

THE NIXON ADMINISTRATION ★ 1969 – 1974

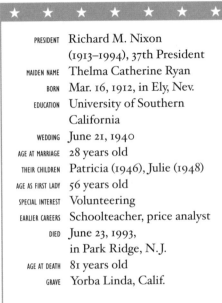

PRESIDENT	Richard M. Nixon (1913–1994), 37th President
MAIDEN NAME	Thelma Catherine Ryan
BORN	Mar. 16, 1912, in Ely, Nev.
EDUCATION	University of Southern California
WEDDING	June 21, 1940
AGE AT MARRIAGE	28 years old
THEIR CHILDREN	Patricia (1946), Julie (1948)
AGE AS FIRST LADY	56 years old
SPECIAL INTEREST	Volunteering
EARLIER CAREERS	Schoolteacher, price analyst
DIED	June 23, 1993, in Park Ridge, N.J.
AGE AT DEATH	81 years old
GRAVE	Yorba Linda, Calif.

Did You Know?

- The Nixons' younger daughter married in December 1968, some weeks after her father's election victory but before his Inauguration.
- Pat Nixon traveled more extensively than any other First Lady up to that time, visiting some 83 nations in all. She joined her husband for his historic trips to China and the Soviet Union, and she made solo appearances elsewhere, including in South America and Africa.
- Inscribed on Pat Nixon's gravestone are the following words: "Even when people can't speak your language, they can tell if you have love in your heart."

"It takes heart to be in political life."

— Pat Nixon

PARALLELS ECHO BETWEEN THE LIVES of Pat Nixon and her First Lady predecessor. Thelma Catherine Ryan earned an early nickname, too. She became "Pat" for having been born on the eve of St. Patrick's Day. Like Lady Bird Johnson, Pat's mother died during her youth. (Katharine Halberstadt Bender Ryan died when Pat was 13.) By 17 Pat had become an orphan following the death of her father, William Ryan, a coal miner and farmer. A hardscrabble existence followed, and only after great effort and economizing was she able to put herself through college.

The future First Lady met her husband-to-be when the two of them were cast in a community theater production. Like Lyndon B. Johnson, Richard M. Nixon proposed to his wife upon meeting her. Their courtship lasted longer (two years), but it eventually led to marriage, and a similar career track put this couple into the White House, too.

Pat strengthened the tradition of recent First Ladies supporting a national cause. Her efforts went toward several, most notably the promotion of community volunteer work. When scandals began to cloud Nixon's administration, she stood by her husband. "I believe in him, and I am proud of his accomplishments," she said. When the President eventually went on television to announce that he would resign from office, Pat was at his side, albeit almost in tears, with other supportive family members.

Pat Nixon (left page) helped organize the first outdoor wedding at the White House when her daughter, Patricia, wed Edward Cox in a June 1971 ceremony in the Rose Garden. The proud parents appeared arm-in-arm (above) during the event.

Felix de Cossio

Betty Ford

PRESIDENT	Gerald R. Ford (1913–present), 38th President
MAIDEN NAME	Elizabeth Anne Bloomer
BORN	Apr. 18, 1918, in Chicago, Ill.
WEDDING	Oct. 15, 1948
AGE AT MARRIAGE	30 years old
THEIR CHILDREN	Michael (1950), John (1952), Steven (1956), Susan (1957)
AGE AS FIRST LADY	56 years old
SPECIAL INTEREST	Handicapped children
EARLIER CAREERS	Model, professional dancer, dance teacher
PREVIOUS MARRIAGE	William C. Warren, 1942 (ended in divorce)

Did You Know?

• Betty Ford made public her addiction to alcohol and painkillers, just as she had previously made public her breast cancer diagnosis. She hoped her honesty would help others face issues not regularly discussed at the time. She established the Betty Ford Clinic to help patients deal with similar addictions.

Betty Ford (above) during a speech.

BETTY FORD HAD BARELY ADJUSTED to becoming the wife of a Vice President when her husband was elevated to the office of President. Although Ford had never sought the Presidency, the job was his anyway. His wife, by association, became First Lady, like it or not.

The daughter of William Stephenson Bloomer, a salesman, and Hortense Neahr Bloomer, Betty developed an early interest in modern dance. At one point she trained in New York with the noted choreographer Martha Graham and danced in one of her troupes. When Betty met her husband, she was newly divorced and living back in Michigan. Ford was a 35-year-old bachelor on the brink of his political career. He was actually late for their wedding, showing up with muddy shoes after attending a political rally for himself.

Helping out handicapped children became one of the themes of Betty's activism during her years as First Lady. She had explored this need earlier in life by teaching dance to children with disabilities. She drew on other personal experiences and convictions, too. When breast cancer led to radical surgery soon after her husband became President, Betty used her own example to educate others about an illness that was rarely discussed publicly before then. She hoped her openness would help save lives by promoting the basics of early detection.

Betty Ford (left page) advocated for increased women's rights during her husband's Presidency. She encouraged Gerald R. Ford to name the first woman to the U.S. Supreme Court (he named a man instead). She lobbied states to ratify the Equal Rights Amendment (some did, but not enough to make it law). She spoke out in favor of reproductive choice, too, a freedom only recently granted by the Supreme Court. She joined her husband, a decorated Navy veteran, as he piloted a riverboat during a presidential photo opportunity (above).

Rosalynn Carter

THE CARTER ADMINISTRATION ★ *1977 – 1981*

PRESIDENT	Jimmy Carter (1924–present), 39th President
MAIDEN NAME	Rosalynn Smith
BORN	Aug. 18, 1927, in Botsford, Ga.
EDUCATION	Georgia Southwestern College
WEDDING	July 7, 1946
AGE AT MARRIAGE	18 years old
THEIR CHILDREN	John (1947), James (1950), Jeffrey (1952), Amy (1968)
AGE AS FIRST LADY	49 years old
SPECIAL INTEREST	Mental illness
EARLIER CAREER	Bookkeeper for family peanut business

Did You Know?

- Rosalynn Carter's memoir of her years in the White House—*First Lady from Plains*—became a best-seller.
- In retirement Rosalynn works alongside her husband to promote issues of social justice through the Carter Center in Atlanta, Ga. They advocate for democratic elections, human rights, international health care, mental health programs, and other humanitarian needs.
- Both of the Carters volunteer to build homes with Habitat for Humanity.

Rosalynn Carter (above) during a trip overseas.

ROSALYNN CARTER HELPED HER HUSBAND Jimmy Carter overcome his relative obscurity and win election to the White House. Their divide-and-conquer strategy, with each person campaigning separately, helped them double their exposure. It also expanded the trend of increased involvement in campaigns by political spouses, especially those married to presidential hopefuls.

Rosalynn was the third of the past four First Ladies to grow up in a single-parent home. Her father, a mechanic and school bus driver named Wilburn Edgar Smith, died when she was 13. Her mother, Allethea Murray Smith, supported her family as a seamstress and depended heavily on Rosalynn, as the eldest of four children, for help. Although Rosalynn and her future husband had grown up as neighbors in the same small town (Rosalynn had even been best friends with Carter's sister), the two did not become sweethearts until years later. Carter, at home on leave from the U.S. Naval Academy, told his mother after their first date: "She's the girl I want to marry." By the next year he had.

Like her predecessor, Rosalynn worked for passage of the Equal Rights Amendment. She chose mental health as her advocacy issue, serving as honorary chair of a Commission on Mental Health established by the President.

A youthful 53 when she left the White House, Rosalynn joined her husband in one of the most active and influential retirements of a former Chief Executive and First Lady.

Rosalynn Carter (left page) played a more active role than any previous First Lady in the policy of her husband's administration. She represented the government as an official spokesperson to foreign governments (a First Lady first) and sat in on Cabinet meetings at times (another first). The Carters broke with precedent on Inauguration Day and walked from the U.S. Capitol building to the White House (above). The Clintons repeated this gesture during the 1990s.

EACH
HER OWN
WOMAN

★ *1981 – present* ★

1981

President Ronald Reagan appointed Sandra Day O'Connor as the first woman justice on the U.S. Supreme Court. She met with lawmakers on Capitol Hill (above) prior to her unanimous confirmation.

1982

The Vietnam Veterans Memorial, designed by 21-year-old Asian-American Maya Lin, was dedicated in Washington, D.C.

1982

The Equal Rights Amendment, first introduced to Congress in 1923 and passed by both houses in 1972, failed to win ratification by falling five states short of the required passage by 38 state legislatures.

1983

Sally Ride became the first American woman in outer space during a six-day mission on the space shuttle Challenger.

The role of First Lady became increasingly personalized as the 20th century drew to a close. Modern presidential wives wielded considerable influence within the White House and beyond. Each one set her own boundaries, tone, and goals while working to reconcile the traditional role of wife with expanding opportunities for women. Personal choice and preference mattered more than precedents set by former First Ladies. By the start of the 21st century, the horizon was within view where a woman might become President and her husband serve as helpmate on the job.

1987

The U.S. Congress declared March "Women's History Month" to promote greater knowledge of women and their history.

1987

Wilma Mankiller successfully campaigned to become the first Native American woman to lead a modern Indian nation.

1999

More than 90,000 spectators watched the United States beat China in the final soccer game of the Women's World Cup. It was the largest crowd ever for a women's sporting event.

2000

Voters elected a record number of women to Congress: 13 Senators and 61 Representatives. Four years later First Lady Hillary Rodham Clinton (above) became New York's newest U.S. Senator.

Nancy Reagan

THE REAGAN ADMINISTRATION ★ *1981 – 1989*

PRESIDENT	Ronald Reagan (1911–2004), 40th President
MAIDEN NAME	Nancy Davis (born Anne Frances Robbins)
BORN	July 6, 1921, in New York. N.Y.
EDUCATION	Smith College
WEDDING	Mar. 4, 1952
AGE AT MARRIAGE	30 years old
THEIR CHILDREN	Patti (1952), Ronald (1958)
AGE AS FIRST LADY	59 years old
SPECIAL INTEREST	Discouraging illegal drug use
EARLIER CAREER	Actress
PRESIDENT'S OTHER WIVES	Jane Wyman (1914–present), first wife (married Jan. 24, 1940; divorced July 19, 1949)
OTHER CHILDREN	Maureen (1941), Michael (1945, adopted)

Did You Know?

• Nancy Reagan (then Nancy Davis) debuted on Broadway in a play called *Ramshackle Inn*. The 22-year-old actress spoke three lines. Five years later she passed a screen test and moved to Hollywood.

"My life really began when I married my husband," observed Nancy Reagan (above during the later years of their partnership).

THE WOMAN WHO BECAME KNOWN AS Nancy Reagan started life with a completely different name—Anne Frances Robbins—a name she rarely used. Her family quickly nicknamed her "Nancy," effectively changing her first name. Her last name changed some years after her parents were divorced. Her biological father was an auto salesman named Kenneth Robbins. Her mother, an actress named Edith Luckett Robbins, eventually remarried. Edith's second husband, a neurosurgeon named Loyal Davis, went on to adopt Nancy during her teen years.

Nancy pursued acting as a career, too, majoring in it at Smith College. She acted on Broadway and made 11 films in Hollywood. She met actor Ronald Reagan during their years in the movie business after consulting with him on a union matter. They were married a few years later. Reagan's acting career led him to politics and, at an older age than any of his predecessors, to the White House. His tenure was marred in its early months by an assassination attempt. Nancy turned to an astrologer for advice on the safety of the President's travel plans. This dependence as well as her attempts to influence policy were criticized when they became publicly known later on. As First Lady she encouraged young people to "just say no" to using illegal drugs.

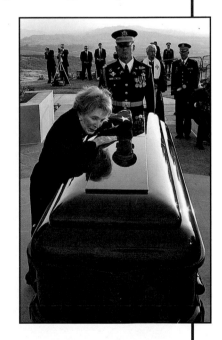

During retirement Reagan developed Alzheimer's disease (which causes memory loss). Nancy devoted herself to him as caregiver, just as she had as wife, until his death ten years later.

Nancy Reagan (left page) headed a week-long program of memorials for her husband after his death in 2004. Herself 82, she traveled coast to coast with his body, finally bidding her husband goodbye at his California burial site (above).

Barbara Bush

THE GEORGE BUSH ADMINISTRATION ★ 1989 – 1993

PRESIDENT	George Bush (1924–present), 41st President
MAIDEN NAME	Barbara Pierce
BORN	June 8, 1925, in Bronx, N.Y.
EDUCATION	Smith College
WEDDING	Jan. 6, 1945
AGE AT MARRIAGE	19 years old
THEIR CHILDREN	George W. (1946), Robin (1949), John (1953), Neil (1955), Marvin (1956), Dorothy (1959)
AGE AS FIRST LADY	63 years old
SPECIAL INTEREST	Promoting literacy

Did You Know?

- Barbara Bush is a distant relative of President Franklin Pierce.
- George Bush and Barbara Pierce fell in love at first sight. She later observed that she had married the first man she kissed.
- George and Barbara Bush have been married longer than any other presidential couple.

As a young woman (above) the future First Lady attended prestigious Smith College in Massachusetts. She dropped out her sophomore year to marry.

HISTORY REPEATED ITSELF WHEN Barbara Bush became First Lady. Just like Abigail Adams, she was the wife of a two-term Vice President turned one-term President. And like Abigail, her eldest son would eventually become President, too. This wife of one President and mother of another grew up outside New York City in the suburban community of Rye, New York. Her parents were a magazine publisher named Marvin Pierce and his wife Pauline Robinson Pierce.

Barbara met her future husband at a holiday dance when she was 16 and he was 17. As newlyweds the pair lived together in Connecticut while George Bush attended Yale University. Then they began a string of more than two dozen moves as Bush's careers took them to Texas, the East Coast, and abroad.

When they reached the White House, Barbara was 63 years old, making her the oldest woman to take on the duties of First Lady. (Anna Harrison was a year older when her husband became President, but she did not accompany him to the White House.) Barbara threw her support behind a number of causes, most notably literacy, the ability of people to read. She donated the sizeable profits from the best-seller *Millie's Book* (which she wrote while First Lady from the point of view of the family dog) to the cause. She promoted AIDS awareness, Head Start, and the needs of senior citizens and the homeless, too. "If it worries you, then you've got to do something about it," she said.

Barbara Bush (left page and above with George Bush) earned the nickname "the silver fox" from her children after her hair turned prematurely white. As First Lady she rarely commented on policy matters. Therefore she made news when she twice disagreed with the President in public, once by supporting women's reproductive freedom and, on another occasion, by objecting to laws that permitted the sale of military assault weapons.

Hillary Rodham Clinton

THE CLINTON ADMINISTRATION ★ 1993 – 2001

PRESIDENT	William Jefferson Clinton (1946–present), 42nd President
MAIDEN NAME	Hillary Diane Rodham
BORN	Oct. 25, 1947, in Park Ridge, Ill.
EDUCATION	Wellesley College, Yale Law School
WEDDING	Oct. 11, 1975
AGE AT MARRIAGE	27 years old
THEIR CHILDREN	Chelsea (1980)
AGE AS FIRST LADY	45 years old
SPECIAL INTEREST	Children's rights
EARLIER CAREER	Lawyer
LATER CAREER	U.S. Senator
ASSISTING FIRST LADY	Chelsea Clinton

Did You Know?

• Hillary Rodham Clinton grew up in a Republican household. In 1964, as a high school senior, she was a "Goldwater girl" during the contest between Barry Goldwater and Lyndon B. Johnson. By 1968 her politics had turned to the Democratic party and the candidacy of Eugene McCarthy.

> "The challenge that faces...us now is to practice politics as the art of making possible what appears impossible."
>
> — Hillary Rodham, *senior class speaker, commencement ceremonies, Wellesley College, 1969*

HILLARY CLINTON WAS THE FIRST BABY BOOMER First Lady, that is, the first to have been born following World War II. During her eight years as First Lady, she combined the commitment of Eleanor Roosevelt with the style of Jacqueline Kennedy—two predecessors whom she greatly admired. She set new precedents for combining career, marriage, and family.

Hugh Rodham and Dorothy Howell Rodham encouraged their oldest child and only daughter to study hard and imagine any career for herself. This daughter of a drapery business owner and a homemaker followed her parents' advice. Hillary was president of her senior high school class and a member of the National Honor Society. She chose to attend prestigious Wellesley College, majored in political science, and graduated with high honors. Classmates chose her to represent them as the first senior speaker at their commencement ceremonies. Hillary progressed from Wellesley to Yale Law School, making her the first First Lady to earn an advanced degree.

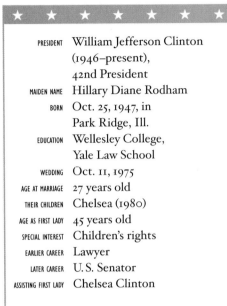

Living History
Hillary Rodham Clinton

It was at Yale that Hillary met her future husband. She introduced herself to William Jefferson "Bill" Clinton after they kept eying one another at the law library. "If you're going to keep looking at me, and I'm going to keep looking back, we at least ought to know each other," she suggested. So began their romantic and political partnership. In her studies, Hillary took a particular interest in family law and

---

After marrying, Hillary continued to use her maiden name instead of adopting her husband's. The decision became controversial (even though the practice was gaining in popularity), and she eventually blended the names as Hillary Rodham Clinton (above, on the cover of her First Lady memoir). Hillary broke precedents on entering the White House (when she set up her own office in the President's West Wing headquarters) and after leaving it (by wearing pants for her official portrait, left page).

Hillary Rodham Clinton is the first First Lady to maintain a career throughout most of her married life. Soon after graduating from law school, she worked on the legal team (above left) advising Congressional Representatives about the case for impeaching President Richard M. Nixon. After her marriage to Bill Clinton, she practiced law in Arkansas. Then, while still First Lady, she launched her candidacy for the U.S. Senate (above right, on the campaign trail during 2000).

the rights of children. As a law student she interned with the Children's Defense Fund. After her graduation she served as one of only three women (on a 41-member team) who advised the House Judiciary Committee about the possible impeachment of President Richard M. Nixon.

A continuing interest in Bill Clinton led Hillary to take a teaching post at the law school of the University of Arkansas where her future husband taught, too. By the next year she and Clinton had married. Soon afterward her husband became first the Attorney General and then the Governor of Arkansas. Even then Hillary continued to work, moving from the law school to become partner in a major law firm. She was so well regarded in her work there that she was twice named to a prestigious list of the "100 Most Influential Lawyers in America." She regularly made more money each year than her husband. When the Clintons' only daughter was born, Hillary managed to juggle her career, her duties as wife of a public official, and the role of mother. Her efforts coincided with a growing trend among young women to combine multiple roles into one lifestyle.

When the Clintons moved to the White House, Hillary left behind her post at the law firm. She did not abandon her professional interests, however,

and she became a more active participant in the government than any First Lady to date. She offered her expertise and counsel to the President and other staff members. At the President's request she chaired a task force that studied ways to reform the nation's health care system.

This effort tested the limits of a First Lady's role in setting policy, and in the end the group's recommendations failed to gain approval in Congress. Although Hillary tempered her style along the way (eventually she moved out of the West Wing office she had established as a new First Lady, for example), she continued to be a central figure in her husband's administration. She traveled widely on his behalf, at times bringing along their teenage daughter, Chelsea. She became an international champion for the rights of women and children. Taking a cue from Eleanor Roosevelt, she established her own weekly newspaper column, "Talking It Over."

Hillary weathered charges of political misconduct (they proved to be false), defended her husband during his own charges of misconduct (also declared false), and stood by him when deceit over a romantic affair contributed to Bill Clinton's Congressional impeachment and trial (he was acquitted). She persevered on her own course,

"Our lives are a mixture of different roles. Most of us are doing the best we can to find whatever the right balance is....
For me, that balance is family, work, and service."

— Hillary Clinton, *1992 presidential campaign*

setting precedents small (like declaring the White House a smoke-free zone) and large (such as testifying on Capitol Hill in support of legislation).

Then Hillary broke the greatest precedent of all. In February 2000 she made official an idea that she had considered for months: She would run for elected office. No other First Lady had ever attempted such a step, either before or after serving. Hillary's objective was to become a U.S. Senator, and she spent much of the rest of her husband's Presidency working toward that goal. Chelsea even stepped in occasionally for her mother as hostess when the demands of campaigning competed with Hillary's social duties as First Lady.

On Election Day 2000, Hillary was able to proclaim that after "62 counties, 16 months, three debates, two opponents, and six black pantsuits" she had succeeded. First Lady Hillary Rodham Clinton completed her months in the White House as Senator-elect for the state of New York. Bill Clinton's retirement marked the beginning of a new career for his wife.

Despite her junior status in the U.S. Senate, Hillary became a visible (and, at times, controversial) presence on issues like the war in Iraq, national defense, health care, and voter fraud. Her strong reelection bid in 2006 left Republicans scrambling to find a suitable challenger. Speculation that she might someday run for President is perennial. Senator Clinton splits her time between Washington, D.C., and her home in New York State.

Hillary Rodham Clinton's political career began in January 2001 (above left, Hillary being sworn in with her husband and daughter) just as Bill Clinton's Presidency drew to a close. No other First Lady has ever run for elected office, and none has stepped away from the White House to pursue a career. Hillary is the first woman Senator from New York State (above right, at work on Capitol Hill during 2006). Only 26 other women had ever served in the U.S. Senate when she joined Congress.

Laura Bush

PRESIDENT **George W. Bush**
(1946–present),
43rd President

MAIDEN NAME **Laura Welch**

BORN **Nov. 4, 1946, in Midland, Tex.**

EDUCATION **Southern Methodist University; University of Texas**

WEDDING **Nov. 5, 1977**

AGE AT MARRIAGE **31 years old**

THEIR CHILDREN **Jenna and Barbara, twins (1981)**

AGE AS FIRST LADY **54 years old**

SPECIAL INTEREST **Promoting literacy**

EARLIER CAREERS **Schoolteacher, librarian**

Did You Know?

• Ronald Reagan instituted the tradition of weekly radio addresses early in his Presidency. First Ladies Nancy Reagan and Hillary Rodham Clinton participated with their husbands in some radio speeches, but Laura Bush was the first First Lady to present an entire weekly radio speech by herself. She spoke two months after the September 11th terrorist attacks.

In 2002 Laura Bush appeared on Sesame Street (above) to promote reading and literacy.

HAD LAURA WELCH NOT ATTENDED the outdoor barbecue where she met her future husband, she might still be a school librarian. Instead she became the First Lady of Texas when George W. Bush won the Governor's seat there. Some two decades later, following her husband's election bid in 2000, she became the First Lady of the Land in the nation's capital.

During her childhood, all Laura had wanted to do was become a schoolteacher. She grew up as the only child of Harold Bruce Welch, a home builder, and Jenna Louise Hawkins Welch, his bookkeeper. Laura made good on her childhood ambition after she graduated from Southern Methodist University in 1968. Her first job was teaching reading in an integrated public school in Dallas. Laura's love of books prompted her to return to school and gain a master's degree in library science in Austin from the University of Texas in 1973. She worked briefly at a public library in Houston. Her interest in education led her back to Austin, however, and a post as librarian for a local elementary school.

Then Laura visited her hometown and attended the barbecue party where she met George W. Bush. The two had almost crossed paths before, having attended the same junior high school at one point. They lived in the same apartment complex during her Houston stay, too, but never met there. This time they connected. By the next evening they were on their first date together (playing miniature golf), and within three months they were married. Four years later they added twins to their family. Their daughters are fraternal, not identical, twins and are named for their grandmothers, one of whom was First Lady Barbara Bush.

Laura and George W. Bush like to laugh about how she agreed to marry him only if she would never have to give political

Laura Bush (left page) has turned her lifelong love of reading into a career of activism. As First Lady she makes the promotion of literacy programs one of her most prominent activities.

"I think I temper [George's boisterous] personality, but I also think that he makes life much more exciting for me."

— Laura Bush

speeches for her future husband. Yet within a short while Laura had stepped from the quiet career of librarian onto a path that eventually led to the White House. "So much for political promises," Laura joked years later in one of the countless speeches she has given during her husband's political career.

Even though she may not sit behind a librarian's desk any longer, Laura remains committed to her love of books. As a Governor's wife, and now as First Lady, she has championed the importance of books and literacy. In Texas she established a Texas Book Festival that raised some $1 million in funding for state libraries. Now her National Book Festival promotes the importance of reading, too.

From her premarriage desire to avoid public speaking, she went on to become the first First

Lady to speak in the President's place during his weekly scheduled radio address. Laura chose to talk about life for women in Afghanistan. She noted: "Fighting brutality against women and children is not the expression of a specific culture; it is the acceptance of our common humanity—a commitment shared by people of good will on every continent....The fight against terrorism is also a fight for the rights and dignity of women."

Unanticipated events may overtake the plans of First Ladies just as they do for Presidents. Following the September 11th terrorist attacks of 2001, Laura found herself serving as a comfort figure to the nation. Her background in education gave her insights into the fears that the attacks would create among young people, and she offered advice on how parents might reassure

Laura Bush made a campaign stop (above, left) on behalf of President George W. Bush on the final day of his 2004 reelection bid. She was joined by their daughters Barbara (at left) and Jenna Bush (center). During his second term of office, President Bush gave his wife a Scottish terrier puppy as a birthday present. She named the pup Miss Beazley, borrowing the name of a character (Uncle Beazley) from the children's book The Enormous Egg. *Miss Beazley (above, right, with the First Lady) met the family dog Barney soon after.*

"When I was a child, one of my most prized possessions was my library card," stated Laura Bush when presiding over a conference about libraries at the White House during her husband's first term of office. "That card was my passport to visit a little house on the prairie, sail across the ocean on a whaling ship, or travel back in time." Laura's lifelong love of reading has led her to promote reading through classroom visits (above), public speaking, and grant support from the Laura Bush Foundation for America's Libraries.

their children. She sought to console the nation with her calming statements. In the months and years that followed, Laura made a number of trips to nations in the Middle East—including Afghanistan, Egypt, Jordan, and Israel—in an effort to reinforce peaceful relations between other countries and the U.S.

Nonetheless Laura has focused most of her energies as First Lady on matters of importance closer to home. In addition to literacy, she has spoken in support of women's health issues (such as breast cancer detection), the arts, early childhood education, Alzheimer's disease, historic

preservation, conserving regional landscapes, and volunteerism. Although Laura has not played a visible role in policy-making, her husband counts on her for advice and feedback. Throughout their marriage she has blended attention to her favorite issues with support for her husband's career and devotion to her family.

Barbara Bush has commended her daughter-in-law for having "a great philosophy in life—you can either like it or not, so you might as well like it." In addition Laura shares a belief held by many other First Ladies: If you work to make a difference, you will have done well with your life.

"The role of First Lady is whatever the First Lady wants it to be."

— Laura Bush

Facts at a Glance

The women recognized in *Our Country's First Ladies* represent the 39 wives who lived during at least some of their husbands' Presidencies, the deceased wives of the four men who were widowers throughout their terms of office, and the niece who served as First Lady for the only President who never married, James Buchanan. For Presidents with multiple marriages, earlier or subsequent wives who fall outside of this definition are acknowledged in the essay text only and are not counted in the statistics that follow. Lists of First Ladies below are presented in chronological order by their husbands' Presidencies; adult names are used throughout.

BIRTHPLACES ⟿ The 44 First Ladies were born in 19 states and one foreign country. New York State gave birth to the most First Ladies, nine. Ohio and Virginia are next with six apiece. Louisa Adams was the only foreign-born First Lady (in London, England). Her American parents were living abroad at the time.

BACKGROUNDS ⟿ More future First Ladies (nine) grew up as daughters of farmers and planters than any other profession. Another six were raised by lawyers and judges. Five had ministers for fathers. Others had fathers who were political figures, bankers, and members of the armed services, among other professions. Few mothers of First Ladies held jobs outside the home. Those who did include Rosalynn Carter's mother (who was a seamstress), Nancy Reagan's (an actress), and Laura Bush's (a bookkeeper).

EDUCATION ⟿ Anna Harrison was the first First Lady to attend a formal school. Lucretia Garfield was the first to attend college. Ten First Ladies have graduated from college. They are: Lucy Hayes (1850), Frances Cleveland (1885), Grace Coolidge (1902), Lou Hoover (1898), Jacqueline Kennedy (1951), Lady Bird Johnson (1933), Pat Nixon (1937), Nancy Reagan (1943), Hillary Rodham Clinton (1969), and Laura Bush (1968). Two First Ladies have earned graduate degrees. They are Hillary Rodham Clinton (in law) and Laura Bush (in library science).

CAREERS ⟿ Abigail Fillmore was the first future First Lady to hold a job outside of the home. She taught school while she was still single. Lucretia Garfield was the first to hold a job after marriage (also as a schoolteacher). Subsequent First Ladies have, among other jobs, helped in their husband's offices (Sarah Polk, Florence Harding, Bess Truman, and Lady Bird Johnson), worked in journalism and media (Jacqueline Kennedy and Lady Bird Johnson), danced professionally (Betty Ford), acted (Nancy Reagan), been a lawyer (Hillary Rodham Clinton), and served as a librarian (Laura Bush). Hillary Rodham Clinton became the first to pursue a profession while her husband was still President when she ran for the U.S. Senate in 2004 (and won).

WEDDINGS ⟿ The youngest First Lady bride was Eliza Johnson, who married at age 16. The oldest, at age 43, was Edith Wilson; it was her second marriage. The oldest first-time bride was Bess Truman, age 34. Frances Cleveland was one of three women to marry sitting Presidents. The others were Julia Tyler (in 1844) and Edith Wilson (1915). Only the Clevelands' wedding, which took place in 1886, was held at the White House.

MARRIAGES ⟿ Thirty-seven First Ladies had only one marriage. Seven had been married before they wed future or sitting Presidents. Four of these earlier marriages had ended with the death of the first spouse (for Martha Washington, Martha Jefferson, Dolley Madison, and Edith Wilson). Three had resulted in divorce (for Rachel Jackson, Florence Harding, and Betty Ford). John and Julia Tyler had the greatest difference in age of a presidential couple, 30 years. Martin and Hannah Van

First Ladies Landmarks

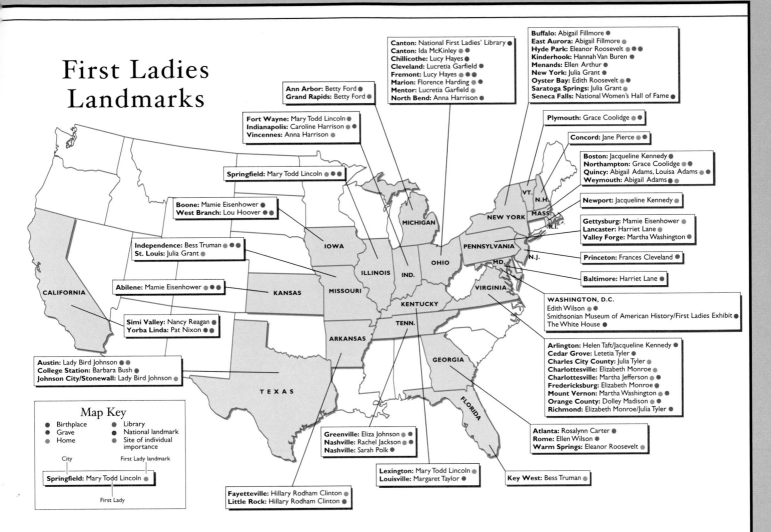

Canton: National First Ladies' Library ●
Canton: Ida McKinley ● ●
Chillicothe: Lucy Hayes ●
Cleveland: Lucretia Garfield ●
Fremont: Lucy Hayes ● ● ●
Marion: Florence Harding ● ●
Mentor: Lucretia Garfield ●
North Bend: Anna Harrison ●

Buffalo: Abigail Fillmore ● ●
East Aurora: Abigail Fillmore ●
Hyde Park: Eleanor Roosevelt ● ● ●
Kinderhook: Hannah Van Buren ●
Menands: Ellen Arthur ●
New York: Julia Grant ●
Oyster Bay: Edith Roosevelt ●
Saratoga Springs: Julia Grant ●
Seneca Falls: National Women's Hall of Fame ●

Ann Arbor: Betty Ford ●
Grand Rapids: Betty Ford ●

Plymouth: Grace Coolidge ● ●

Concord: Jane Pierce ● ●

Fort Wayne: Mary Todd Lincoln ●
Indianapolis: Caroline Harrison ● ●
Vincennes: Anna Harrison ●

Boston: Jacqueline Kennedy ●
Northampton: Grace Coolidge ● ●
Quincy: Abigail Adams, Louisa Adams ● ●
Weymouth: Abigail Adams ●

Springfield: Mary Todd Lincoln ● ● ●

Newport: Jacqueline Kennedy ●

Boone: Mamie Eisenhower ●
West Branch: Lou Hoover ● ●

Gettysburg: Mamie Eisenhower ●
Lancaster: Harriet Lane ●
Valley Forge: Martha Washington ●

Independence: Bess Truman ● ● ●
St. Louis: Julia Grant ●

Princeton: Frances Cleveland ●

Abilene: Mamie Eisenhower ● ● ●

Baltimore: Harriet Lane ●

WASHINGTON, D.C.
Edith Wilson ● ●
Smithsonian Museum of American History/First Ladies Exhibit ●
The White House ●

Simi Valley: Nancy Reagan ●
Yorba Linda: Pat Nixon ● ●

Arlington: Helen Taft/Jacqueline Kennedy ●
Cedar Grove: Letetia Tyler ●
Charles City County: Julia Tyler ●
Charlottesville: Elizabeth Monroe ●
Charlottesville: Martha Jefferson ●
Fredericksburg: Elizabeth Monroe ●
Mount Vernon: Martha Washington ●
Orange County: Dolley Madison ● ●
Richmond: Elizabeth Monroe/Julia Tyler ●

Austin: Lady Bird Johnson ● ●
College Station: Barbara Bush ●
Johnson City/Stonewall: Lady Bird Johnson ●

Atlanta: Rosalynn Carter ●
Rome: Ellen Wilson ●
Warm Springs: Eleanor Roosevelt ●

Map Key
- ● Birthplace
- ● Grave
- ● Home
- ● Library
- ● National landmark
- ● Site of individual importance

City   First Lady landmark

Springfield: Mary Todd Lincoln ●

First Lady

Greenville: Eliza Johnson ● ●
Nashville: Rachel Jackson ● ●
Nashville: Sarah Polk ●

Lexington: Mary Todd Lincoln ●
Louisville: Margaret Taylor ●

Key West: Bess Truman ●

Fayetteville: Hillary Rodham Clinton ●
Little Rock: Hillary Rodham Clinton ●

Buren were the closest in age; only 93 days separated their birthdates. The marriage of George and Barbara Bush has lasted longer than any other presidential couple; in 1999 they eclipsed the previous record of 54 years that had been set by John and Abigail Adams. Of the 39 First Ladies who survived to witness their husbands' presidencies, Edith Wilson had the shortest marriage (eight years). Two First Ladies married again following the deaths of their presidential husbands (Frances Cleveland and Jacqueline Kennedy).

CHILDREN ⌐ Only two First Ladies never had children. They are Rachel Jackson and Sarah Polk. Others had as few as one child (Bess Truman and Hillary Rodham Clinton) or as many as ten children who survived infancy (Anna Harrison). Three First Ladies only had children from prior, non-presidential marriages (Martha Washington, Dolley Madison, and Florence Harding). Only one, Martha Jefferson, had children by both a President and a former spouse.

AGES ⌐ Women were as young as 21 (Frances Cleveland) and as old as 64 (Barbara Bush) when they began serving as First Lady. Bess Truman lived longer than any other First Lady; she was 97 years old when she died. Martha Jefferson, who died at age 33, lived the shortest life of the women who are recognized here as First Ladies.

DEATH IN OFFICE ⌐ Three First Ladies died during their husband's Presidencies. They are: Letitia Tyler (1842), Caroline Harrison (1892), and Ellen Wilson (1914).

RETIREMENTS ⌐ Frances Cleveland lived longer than any other First Lady after leaving the White House, 51 years. Abigail Fillmore lived the shortest period, 26 days. Sarah Polk outlived her presidential spouse by the longest span of time, 42 years. Eliza Johnson died the closest in time to a spouse and former President, 168 days. Sixteen First Ladies have outlived their retired husbands; seven have predeceased them.

Resources & Credits

References and Related Resources

Anthony, Carl Sferrazza. *America's First Families*. New York: Simon & Schuster, 2000.

_____. *First Ladies: The Saga of the Presidents' Wives and Their Power, 1789-1961*. New York: Perennial, HarperCollins Publishers, 1990.

_____. *First Ladies: The Saga of the Presidents' Wives and Their Power, 1961-1990*. New York: Perennial, HarperCollins Publishers, 1993.

_____. *This Elevated Position: A Catalogue and Guide to the National First Ladies' Library and the Importance of First Lady History*. Canton, Ohio: National First Ladies' Library, 2003.

Baker, Jean H. *Mary Todd Lincoln: A Biography*. New York: W.W. Norton & Company, 1987.

Boller, Jr., Paul F. *Presidential Wives*. New York: Oxford University Press, 1998 (second edition).

Caroli, Betty Boyd. *The First Ladies*. Garden City, New York: Guild America Books (by arrangement with Oxford University Press), 2001 (third edition).

DeGregorio, William A. *The Complete Book of U.S. Presidents*. New York: Gramercy Books, 2002 (fifth edition).

Gould, Lewis L. *American First Ladies: Their Lives and Their Legacy*. London: Routledge, 2001 (second edition).

Kane, Joseph Nathan, Janet Podell, and Steven Anzovin. *Facts about the Presidents*. New York: H.W. Wilson Company, 2001 (seventh edition).

Klapthor, Margaret Brown. *The First Ladies*. Washington, D.C.: White House Historical Association and National Geographic Society, 1999 (ninth edition).

Pearce, Lorraine. *The White House: An Historic Guide*. Washington, D.C.: White House Historical Association and National Geographic Society, 1999 (20th edition).

Wead, Douglas. *All the Presidents' Children*. New York: Atria Books, 2003.

Books for Young Readers

Bausum, Ann. *Our Country's Presidents*. Washington, D.C.: National Geographic Society, 2005 (second edition).

Bausum, Ann. *With Courage and Cloth: Winning the Fight for a Woman's Right to Vote*. Washington, D.C.: National Geographic Society, 2004.

Mayo, Edith P., general editor. *The Smithsonian Book of the First Ladies*. New York: Henry Holt and Company, 1996.

Places to Visit

"First Ladies: Political Role and Public Image," permanent exhibit at the National Museum of American History, Smithsonian Institution, Washington, D.C.

First Ladies National Historic Site, Canton, Ohio

National Women's Hall of Fame, Seneca Falls, N.Y.

The White House, Washington, D.C.

Web Sites

Library of Congress: American Memory— Portraits of the Presidents and First Ladies
http://www.memory.loc.gov/ammem/odmdhtml/preshome.html

Life in the White House
http://www.whitehouse.gov/history/life/

National First Ladies' Library Education and Research Center
http://www.firstladies.org

Smithsonian National Museum of American History—First Ladies: Political Role and Public Image
http://americanhistory.si.edu/youmus/ex12ladi.htm

The White House: First Ladies' Gallery
http://whitehouse.gov/history/firstladies/

Illustrations Credits

Abbreviations:
LC = The Library of Congress
GC = The Granger Collection, New York
NWPA = North Wind Picture Archive
SI = Smithsonian Institution
WHHA (WHC) = White House Historical Association (White House Collection)
t = top, b = bottom, c = center, l = left, r = right

Cover: Top: WHHA (WHC); background (bunting), © Corbis. Bottom, left to right: Fenimore Art Museum, Cooperstown, NY, photo by Richard Walker; WHHA (WHC); WHHA (WHC); WHHA (WHC); Official portrait of Mrs. Laura Bush, White House Photo by Krisanne Johnson.

2-3, John F. Kennedy Library; 6, © Kevin Lamarque/Reuters/Corbis; 9, David Hume Kennerly/Getty Images.

FOUNDING MOTHERS

10 (b, l-r), © Corbis; NWPA; Oil painting by Marian Anderson; NWPA; 11 (b, l-r), NWPA; © Bettmann/Corbis; GC; GC; 12, Hulton Archive/Getty Images; 13, LC; 14, Mount Vernon Ladies' Association; 15 (l), GC; 15 (r), LC; 16, GC; 17, Fenimore Art Museum, Cooperstown, New York, photo by Richard Walker; 18, GC; 20, GC; 21, Hulton Archive/Getty Images; 22, Courtesy of Ash Lawn-Highland, Home of James Monroe, Charlottesville, VA; 23, Courtesy of the James Monroe Museum & Memorial Library, Fredericksburg, VA; 24, GC; 25, © Bettmann/Corbis.

THE AURA OF YOUTH

26 (b, l-r), LC; GC; GC; © Bettmann/Corbis; 27 (b, l-r), GC; GC; Hulton Archive/Getty Images; © Museum of the City of New York/Corbis; 28, WHHA (WHC); 29 (l), WHHA (WHC); 29 (r), Kentucky Department for Libraries and

Archives; 30, GC; 31, WHHA (WHC); 32, President Benjamin Harrison Home, Indianapolis; 33, Francis Vigo Chapter, Daughters of the American Revolution, Vincennes, IN; 34, Reproduced by permission of John Tyler Griffin, great-great-grandson of Letitia and President Tyler; 35, GC; 36, WHHA (WHC); 37, National First Ladies' Library; 38, GC; 39, © Corbis; 40, GC; 41, Photographic History Collection, National Museum of American History, SI; 42, © Bettmann/ Corbis; 43, WHHA (WHC); 44, GC; 45, Photographer unknown, daguerrotype owned by the Pierce Brigade, Concord, NH; 46, GC; 47, National Museum of American History, © SI 2006.

EMERGING POLITICAL PARTNERS
48 (b, l-r), © Corbis; GC; Hulton Archive/Getty Images; LC; 49 (b, l-r), © Underwood & Underwood/Corbis; GC; GC; © Bettmann/Corbis; 50, WHHA (WHC); 51 (l), LC; 51 (r), NWPA; 52, LC; 53, © Chicago Historical Museum, USA/The Bridgeman Art Library; 54, Photographic History Collection, National Museum of American History, SI; 55 (l), Charcoal drawing (possibly by Henry N. Barlow), Andrew Johnson National Historic Site, Greenville, TN; 55 (r), © David J. & Janice L. Frent Collection/Corbis; 56, LC; 57, © Oscar White/Corbis; 58, WHHA (WHC); 59, © Bettmann/Corbis; 60, WHHA (WHC); 61, NWPA; 62, © Corbis; 63, WHHA (WHC); 64, Frances Folsom Cleveland by Anders Leonard Zorn, Oil on canvas, 1899, National Portrait Gallery, SI; gift of Frances Payne, S/NPG.77.124; 65 (l), Photographic History Collection, National Museum of American History, SI; 65 (r), © Bettmann/Corbis; 66, WHHA (WHC); 67, © Corbis; 68, GC; 69, WHHA (WHC).

FIRST LADIES IN NAME AND DEED
70 (b, l-r), © Corbis; © Underwood & Underwood/Corbis; GC; © Bettmann/Corbis; 71 (b, l-r), GC; GC; GC; © Underwood & Underwood/Corbis; 72, WHHA (WHC); 73, LC; 74, WHHA (WHC); 75, LC; 76, WHHA (WHC); 77 (l), © Corbis; 77 (r), Woodrow Wilson House, a National Trust Historic Site, Washington, DC; 78, WHHA (WHC); 79 (l), LC; 79 (r), LC; 80, WHHA (WHC); 81, © Bettmann/ Corbis; 82, WHHA (WHC);

83 (l), © Bettmann/Corbis; 83 (r), © Condé Nast Archive/Corbis; 84, WHHA (WHC); 85 (l), © Corbis; 85 (r), © Corbis;.

LIVES OF PUBLIC SERVICE
86 (b, l-r), *Hattie Caraway* by John Oliver Buckley, U.S. Senate Collection; © Bettmann/Corbis; © Corbis; © Jacques Pavlovsky/Sygma/Corbis; 87 (b, l-r), © Bettmann/Corbis; Alfred Eisenstaedt/Time Life Pictures/Getty Images; © Jim Sugar/Corbis; © Leif Skoogfors/Corbis; 88, WHHA (WHC); 89, GC; 90 (t), Hulton Archive/Getty Images; 90 (b), GC; 91, © Corbis; 92, WHHA (WHC); 93, LC; 94, WHHA (WHC); 95 (l), © David J. & Janice L. Frent Collection/Corbis; 95 (r), © Bettmann Corbis; 96, WHHA (WHC); 97, Time Inc./Time Life Pictures/Getty Images; 98, LC; 99 (b, l-r), John F. Kennedy Library; © Bettmann/Corbis; © Bettmann/ Corbis; 100, WHHA (WHC); 101, © Jay Dickman/Corbis; 102, WHHA (WHC); 103, © J.P. Laffont/Sygma/Corbis; 104, WHHA (WHC); 105 (l), © Bettmann/Corbis; 105 (r), LC; 106, WHHA (WHC);

107 (l), Jimmy Carter Library and Museum; 107 (r), © Corbis.

EACH HER OWN WOMAN
108 (b, l-r), Time Life Pictures/Getty Images; © Richard Hamilton Smith/Corbis; Bill Pierce/Time Life Pictures/Getty Images; © Bettmann/Corbis; 109 (b, l-r), © Bettmann/Corbis; James Schnepf; © Tore Bergsaker/Sygma/Corbis; © Najlah Feanny/Corbis; 110, WHHA (WHC); 111 (l), © Norman Parkinson Limited/Corbis; 111 (r), Kevork Djansezian/Getty Images; 112, WHHA (WHC); 113 (l), George Bush Presidential Library; 113 (r), © Wally McNamee/Corbis; 114, WHHA (WHC); 115, © Reuters/ Corbis; 116 (l), © Wally McNamee/Corbis; 116 (r), © Reuters/Corbis; 117 (l), © Reuters/Corbis; 117 (r), Alex Wong/Getty Images; 118, Official portrait of Mrs. Laura Bush, White House Photo by Krisanne Johnson; 119, Don Emmert/ AFP/Getty Images; 120 (l). © Brooks Kraft/Corbis; 120 (r), Win McNamee/ Getty Images; 121, © Kevin Lamarque/ Reuters/Corbis.

Ann Bausum, the daughter of a history professor, investigates and writes about history for young people. Her book, *With Courage and Cloth,* which chronicles the fight for a woman's right to vote in the U.S., won the 2005 Jane Addams Children's Book Award, and her 2006 book, *Freedom Riders* took off with starred reviews. She is also the author of National Geographic's acclaimed reference book *Our Country's Presidents.* Bausum enjoyed getting to know the First Ladies better. She notes, "Our country's First Ladies were among the heroines of my youth, and the talents, courage, and service of these women continue to fascinate me today. Lady Bird Johnson, First Lady during my childhood, remains a favorite for me, in part because we both share a passion for wildflowers." Ann Bausum lives in Beloit, Wisconsin, with her husband and two sons. Visit her Web site at www.annbausum.com.

Dr. Robert D. Johnston, consultant, is associate professor and director of the Teaching of History Program at the University of Illinois at Chicago. He is also the author of National Geographic's *The Making of America: The History of the United States from 1492 to the Present,* which was named a *School Library Journal* Best Book of the Year. Dr. Johnston lives in Chicago with his wife and two sons.

Index

National Geographic Society

For my own first family —
Dolores, Henry, and David — with love.
— AB

Acknowledgments: The publisher gratefully acknowledges the kind assistance of Carl Sferrazza Anthony, Martha Regula, and other staff members from the National First Ladies' Library; and Harmony Haskins and Hillary Crehan at the White House Historical Association for their generous support of the project. Special thanks go to Robert D. Johnston, Ph.D., of the University of Illinois at Chicago for reviewing and commenting on the text and layout. We also appreciate the assistance of Dr. Nancy Young; Jim Detlefsen of the Hoover Library; and the invaluable contributions of Sue Macy.

The type for this book is set in Hoefler Text.
Design by Ruth Thompson

Printed in the United States of America

Library of Congress Cataloging-in-Publication Data
Bausum, Ann
    Our country's first ladies / Ann Bausum; with a foreword by First Lady Laura Bush
      p. cm.
    Includes bibliographical references and index.
    ISBN-13: 978-1-4263-0006-6 (hardcover)
    ISBN-13: 978-1-4263-0007-3 (library binding)
    1. Presidents' spouses—United States—Biography—I. Title.
E176.2.B38 2007
973.09'9—dc22

Front cover: First Ladies pictured under the photograph of Eleanor Roosevelt are (from left) Abigail Adams, Dolley Madison, Mary Todd Lincoln, Hillary Rodham Clinton, and Laura Bush.

Title page: Jacqueline Kennedy painted this view of the White House during her years as First Lady and presented it to her husband as a gift. He had it hung in the Oval Office where he worked.